keep up the

Take your

Can not wait to have

you on ~~your~~ team

Judson

1-27-21

MILESTONE

THE STRANGEST CONDUIT

MILESTONE

THE STRANGEST

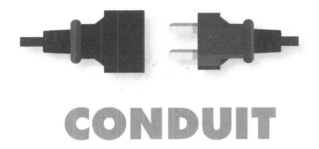

CONDUIT

How a small company made a big impact

GUS ANTOS
MARK ROBISON

Cover Design: **Tyler Holleman** and **RTC**

Writers of the Round Table Press
PO Box 1603, Deerfield, IL 60015
www.roundtablecompanies.com

Lead Editor: **Mary Anna Rodabaugh**
Editors: **James Cook** and **Wendy Strain**
Interior Design: **Sunny DiMartino**
Proofreaders: **Adam Lawrence** and **Carly Cohen**

Printed in the United States of America

First Edition: December 2020
10 9 8 7 6 5 4 3 2 1

Library of Congress Cataloging-in-Publication Data
Milestone: the strangest conduit / Gus Antos and Mark Robison.—1st ed. p. cm.
ISBN Hardcover: 978-1-61066-094-5
ISBN Paperback: 978-1-61066-088-4
ISBN Digital: 978-1-61066-089-1
Library of Congress Control Number: 2020914391

Writers of the Round Table Press and the logo
are trademarks of Writers of the Round Table, Inc.

*We would like to dedicate this book and journey
to all the team members of Milestone past, present, and future.
The biggest blessing of our lives will always be getting to work
with you. Somehow God Blessed us with ALL the BEST people
in the WORLD, go figure! Thank you, Jesus Christ, our Lord and
Savior, for that and so many, many, many other things.*

YOUR CORE VALUES DEFINE OUR CULTURE

FAITH

FAMILY

EXCELLENCE

CONTENTS

About the Authors

The Charge

ACKNOWLEDGMENTS

GUS   To Amanda: thanks for always showing up and being the rock of our family, showing unconditional love. Dean and Alexander: can't wait to see what God has in store for you; thanks for being our greatest blessings (most days!). To Louie and Karen: thanks for providing a great (the best) godly childhood; if everyone was so fortunate, our world would have few problems; LOVE YOU. To Pastor Mike Hankins: almost every good thing in my life has come out of your commitment to following Christ; thank you. To Dr. Ty and Cheryl Davenport: thanks for some of the best, hardest, and most important years of my life; will forever love you guys. Finally, Mark Robison: thank you for taking a chance on a twenty-one-year-old kid—teaching, trusting, and loving me in so many ways; had no idea where this road was headed when I got on it, and still don't; just happy to be on it with you. Most importantly, thank God for His plans and Jesus for His grace.

MARK   First, I want to thank God, for without Him, this story wouldn't have been possible. He put cords in our lives because a three-band cord is stronger than one. Not because we are weak but because we make each other stronger. A rope has thousands of cords bound together. That is what has made Milestone so awesome. I am thankful for the cords in my life. Sabrina (my wife) has demonstrated God's Love, Amanda His Light, Danielle His Strength, Justin His Passion, Gus His Knowledge, and Pastor Mike His Wisdom. There are countless other bonds in my life for which I am truly grateful. Each one has made me who I am today. All we need to succeed in His kingdom is to listen to the Holy Spirit and have the faith to say YES and be thankful He chose us. That's the Story of Milestone.

We would like to thank everyone at Milestone that helped this project come together—specifically, Jackie Watkins, Eric Stewart, Travis Mount, and Ashley Wilkinson for memories, input, proofing, and care. Thank you.

After closing down Masterline Electric, Mark's previous company, Gus and Mark team up to figure out their next business endeavor.

Our first office in Fate, Texas. Here, we operated a race track and U-Haul. At this point, we should've been called "Milestone U-Haul and Racing . . ."

We begin airing commercials on TV. Now all of DFW knows our jingle!

♪♫ **We'll Fix It In A Flash!** ♪♫

Our first family meeting at the Grandy's in Rockwall.

The very first designs for our fleet. A tremendous upgrade from the "Rainbow Truck."

2005

2007

2004

Techs started selling "huge" jobs and averaging $4,000–$5,000 in one week!

2006 | 2008

Having attended a conference in Georgia for home service companies, Gus and Mark realize that they're on the right track. Together, they start a new company called Milestone Electric and the rest is history!

Milestone wins its first CCA award in 2007.

WIN • WIN • WIN

Milestone makes some changes to the overall mission of the company and adopts the motto, WIN – WIN – WIN. This will go on to be the cornerstone of our culture and ethics.

THE
HISTORY OF
MILESTONE

Milestone scores the #41 spot on SMU's "Dallas 100" list.

The whole office participates in National Talk Like a Pirate Day and it was a huge success. Milestone even offered themed desserts.

Milestone begins offering security services with Go Guard Home Security.

Go Guard Security changes its name to Milestone Security and merges in the most epic way possible, a wedding! It was a grand party to celebrate this transition.

2011 | 2012

2009 | 2010

We opened a shop in Euless for our electricians who work near Fort Worth.

Milestone began recognizing acts of kindness towards customers and adopted the term, "give 'em the pickle."

Milestone begins offering HVAC services! Eventually HVAC will surpass Electrical in revenue and become the biggest part of the company.

Milestone moved to Rowlett, providing more space as the company continued to grow.

The year when Milestone really became a stable and flourishing company. Also, the year of epic pranks.

Milestone moves to its new home in Garland due to the tremendous growth of the company!

Milestone officially offers plumbing as a service and changes the name from "Milestone Electric" to "Milestone."

A wellness initiative is introduced as a resource for team members to experience better physical, mental, and financial health.

Milestone makes a very Merry Christmas! Wishes for their customers were granted.

2013 | 2014 | 2015

2016

IAQ services are now offered with an entire department focused solely on indoor air quality.

Our core values are established, defining our culture. Faith, Family, and Excellence are now the foundation for the company.

Milestone Cares begins as an opportunity for team members to actively contribute in our culture of giving.

Milestone encourages healthy living by having the first company walk-a-thon. The office participated in a 30-day challenge to eat healthy.

Featured on the Dallas Morning News "Top 100 places to work 2015" list and earned the #4 spot! We had previously been featured on the list twice, in 2011 and 2014.

The Dallas Morning News

ILTOP 100
PLACES TO WORK 2015

Milestone started a campaign called Stand to Honor to raise 1 million dollars for The Folds of Honor foundation. The goal was met in 11 days.

You thought our techs were clean? You should see our windows. In August 2018, Milestone started offering window cleaning services.

Milestone makes Welborn Garage Doors part of the family, opening our doors to new adventures.

The Hub: Growth is always different, but exciting! After always having our call center down the hall, we made the jump across the street to what we call the "Hub"—an area totally devoted to the culture and success of our customer service team!

The Milestone family extended all the way to Phoenix, AZ in 2019 with Ideal Garage Doors! What an exciting time as we expand beyond North Texas!

2017

WELBORN GARAGE DOORS

2018

2019

Milestone ran it's first drain cleaning call April 2018. Clogged drains don't stand a chance!

Hanks Handyman Services joined the team mid-2019 as a way to provide our customers with excellent services, even for those odd jobs around the house. They are a great addition!

As an extension of Milestone Cares, team members take a trip to Liberia, Africa to install a generator and rewire a local school.

Old Fleet Shop

From old to new. Milestone remodeled it's offices to promote better work flow and culture.

2020

your **FUTURE** is
○ **CREATED** ○
by
WHAT YOU DO

TODAY

not

TOMORROW

Mark Robison Gus Antos Rick Sneed JB Houston
Mike Linger Joe Lambrecht Jeff Meier Fernando
Argueto Alexander Jarred Michael Ames Chad
Blake Ronnie Bell Rosendo Martinez Denise
Faucher Abel Norton Aaron Fleming Jon Trimble
Joshua Smith Eric Stewart Sondra Hierholzer
Randall Macfarland Nancy Robison Aaron
Odom Charles Hurn Sonya Fryar Justin Zimmer-
man Mark Caldwell Laura Burroughs Jeremy
Reynolds Marcus McCloure Ross Sallee Lacy
Paul John Little Roy Hopkins Michael Dark
Joe Serna Brittany Citelli Merle
Gregory Chad Garretson Joshua
Gentry Damon Wilder Humberto
Gonzalez Justin Holt Melissa
Sickel Weston Lather Phillip
Henderson Michael Gravely Kyle
Robison Derek Long James
Bridges Steve Bustos Josh Smith
George Avant Adam Craver Lacy
Paul Stephen Prewitt Luke Por-
ter John Kuykendall Wade Lash-
ley Kurt Chasteen Michael Harder
Jesse Castaneda Mitch Morris
Johnathon Prewitt Adam Jones
Brian Stone Christopher Miller
Jeremy Vinces David Lama Gary
Carlson Jeremy Bowen Danny
Boles Autumn William Whitnie
Giles Erin Coonrod Damon Wilder
Roy Hopkins Leonard Cornelius
Gary Adams Alejandro Chihua-
hua Jason Baxley Cody Thomas

HUMBLE BEGINNINGS

**Humble yourselves before the
Lord, and he will lift you up.**

—James 4:10 NIV

"I feel like I'm supposed to ask if you'll come work for me," Mark told the young man sitting across from him as he bit into his burger. "I'm not sure if I can even pay you, but I feel this is something I have to do."

It was 2004, and Mark Robison owned a small electrical contracting company called Masterline Electric. Business had been challenging. Masterline accrued debt from operation costs and vendor bills. On top of that, the company was facing a hefty tax payment. Mark needed someone to fight from the trenches, and he had a special feeling about Gus. Something inside of Mark urged him to connect with this young man.

Gus Antos was in his early twenties at the time. He worked at a cell phone store in the Dallas–Fort Worth area. Gus hoped to own his own business someday. He had assisted Mark several times in his store, but the two men really got acquainted that afternoon at Joe Willy's, a simple burger-and-fries establishment in Rockwall, Texas.

"I was supposed to be out of town today," Gus said with a smile. "Now I'm really glad I didn't go."

That day, Gus and Mark decided to take a leap of faith. Mark brought on a young, unseasoned man to help resuscitate his struggling business. Gus left his secure job to pursue the surprising offer. Little did they know that casual lunch would be the start of something great.

Within a month, Gus joined the company and dove headfirst into the contracts, billing issues, and overall business development. But two months later, Masterline was still floundering. After several conversations and a lot of prayer, Gus and Mark decided to close Masterline and begin a brand-new company. They wanted to stop relying on the contracting side of the business, with its billing issues and inconsistent workload, and focus on residential electrical services. They agreed to become fifty-fifty partners. It was not an easy decision, but at the time it just made sense.

When deciding on a name, Gus and Mark found inspiration from a line in the Bible: "A milestone to your forefathers." The leap of faith was christened "Milestone Electric."

Gus and Mark began building the new company from the ground up. Mark offered a spot at Milestone to all his former technicians, but many declined. They were not interested in completing residential services. Most technicians flocked to "fancy" jobs working on skyscrapers and innovative corporate projects.

Milestone displays documented errors in their office as a reminder that no obstacle is too big to overcome

Milestone had a humble and challenging start. The company owed the IRS nearly $70,000 in payroll taxes from Masterline. Milestone had a federal tax lien against everything, and Gus and Mark needed to make money fast.

They set up shop in an inexpensive office space located in nearby Fate, Texas. The building was overrun with rats, so Gus and Mark got a few cats to help kill them off. A dirt racetrack sat behind the property. Mark always raced go-karts growing up, so the pair decided to host races on Saturday nights. People would stop by and pay to race around the modest rack. Gus ran a small concession stand, and Mark prepared the track each week. The proceeds were minimal at best, but at least there were proceeds.

First Milestone shop with track behind to help bring in additional revenue

With limited revenue coming in, Gus and Mark then decided to make use of a big parking area next to their office space by renting U-Hauls. About three months into their U-Haul venture, Gus rented a twenty-four-foot U-Haul to a customer. The customer loaded the rig up and headed to California. Not ten minutes after leaving the shop, the customer called saying the truck had broken down on the side of the highway. Gus and Mark had to order another truck from U-Haul, drive it to the broken-down rig, and transfer the contents from one truck to the other—all under the Texas sun, in summer. Sweat soaked everything they had on as the 110-degree heat slowed the process down. As Gus and Mark transferred the customer's load, they both thought in unison, "What in the world are we doing?" It felt so far from what they set out to do with Milestone. They should be sending technicians to homes and building that business, not working as movers on the side of the highway. Gus and Mark were not afraid of hard work, but this venture was not paying off.

Discouraged but determined, Gus and Mark turned to prayer. Their pastor had been talking about prayer and fasting a lot in church. He told the congregation the sacrifice of fasting can bring about humility and complete surrender to God. By going without food and substituting physical sustenance with prayer, one's faith journey can lead to insightful revelations. In January 2005, Gus and Mark decided to go on a three-day fast where they would consume only water. Instead of three meals a day, they came together and prayed things would get better. They prayed for direction. They prayed for strength. They trusted God would support their dream. They surrendered to Him.

It was a challenging time. Gus and Mark were being tested. Gus was living with a friend. Mark's house was on the verge of getting repossessed. Members of their church helped with bills when they could. Milestone took on construction jobs and work for general contractors in addition to the weekend go-kart racing and U-Haul venture. Contracts started getting cancelled left and right, and often the scope of work for certain jobs would change dramatically. In some cases, Milestone didn't have the money to buy materials because the jobs were so big. Despite the prayer and fasting, things turned abruptly for the worse.

Out of nowhere, Sabrina, Mark's wife, took ill. She developed double pneumonia and her body started to shut down. It gave Mark the scare of his life. He was trying to take care of their children, be there for his ailing wife, and help grow a failing company. Bills piled up even more, and Gus and Mark were at the mercy of contractors.

Sabrina stayed in the hospital for three months. During that time, Mark had to step away from Milestone's day-to-day operations. He was still involved but conducted business from Sabrina's hospital room when he could. He trusted Gus to keep things afloat. He prayed for Sabrina's recovery and for hope that everything would turn out all right.

At Masterline, Mark usually managed the employees, and Gus handled the office and marketing. Now Gus had to get into the weeds of every aspect of the operation. He was twenty-one years old and had no clue how to run the daily operations of a business, much less an electrical contracting business.

Mark's team members who stuck with Milestone after the transition from Masterline didn't like Gus's interim leadership role. Mark brought them on, and they trusted him as a leader. The team members felt loyalty to Mark and thought Gus made too many changes in Mark's absence. In their eyes, Gus wasn't a tradesperson, which was true, and they held that against him.

For contracts, Gus would flip through the estimating book in Mark's office and try to make sense of it. No one taught him the operational processes, and Mark couldn't offer that one-on-one training Gus desperately needed. Fortunately, Mark knew some friends from church who were electrical contractors. They were able to help bid and estimate a couple of jobs for Gus until he caught on to the process. It was a small step in the right direction.

To make additional money and build the residential service offering, Milestone started offering after-hours services. If a customer called after hours and Milestone didn't pick up the phone or service the customer that evening, the service call would be free the next day. Gus was frequently on call.

One Tuesday evening, Gus received a request at ten o'clock at night.

"Hi, I need someone to come out tonight. I don't have power at my house," the customer said.

"All right, we'll be right out."

Power outage jobs were great and usually netted several thousand dollars. Gus called a technician. As fate would have it, the tech was unable to attend to the call. Gus would have to service the customer by himself. Remember, Gus was not a contractor.

Gus arrived at the house shortly after 10:30 p.m. "We don't know what is wrong, we just don't have power," the customer told him.

Gus told them he was going to take a look outside, which is where Mark had told him to start his inspection. He planned on calling Mark as soon as he was outside so Mark could walk him through what he was seeing, but the customer followed Gus into the backyard.

"Uh, for your safety, would you mind waiting inside?"

The customer agreed and went back in, and Gus let out a sigh of relief, as now Mark could walk him through the evaluation step-by-step without the customer overhearing.

"Mark, I have a flashlight. What am I looking for?" Gus asked.

After a few questions, Mark figured out what the problem was. The meter base had to be replaced, and Gus would need to order parts for the job to be completed. Confidently, Gus relayed the information to the customer and offered to have Milestone pay for a hotel for the evening until the technicians could come back with the parts the next day. It sounds like a generous offer, but Milestone had to make it. If they did not put the customer in a hotel, they ran the risk of a competing contractor putting in a bid before they could start the job.

Little did they know that God was pushing Milestone toward their current business model. If Gus and Mark stuck with all the cancelled contracts, the U-Haul business, the construction jobs, and even the go-kart racetrack, Milestone wouldn't be the business it is today.

Back in late 2004, a friend of Mark's suggested he and Gus check out a company that was doing something for residential services in Atlanta. Gus and Mark didn't have any money at the time. They wrote a check to the hotel in Atlanta and asked if the hotel would wait to cash the check until they had the funds in place. Mercifully, the hotel agreed, and the check cleared.

The mystery company in Atlanta was called Success Group International (SGI), an organization that teaches individuals how to run a good business, be a good contractor, and implement best principles. The program put members in contact with one thousand other people doing the same type of work. It came with a $12,000 price tag. Gus and Mark were nervous. They would need to find the money somewhere. It was perhaps the scariest decision they ever made. But they knew they had to do it. It felt like the right kind of investment.

Milestone joined the four hundred other SGI members (at the time) as an electrical services company, and eventually grew to become the biggest electrical contractor in the group. SGI taught the team how to be successful and gave Gus and Mark tools to get out of the huge financial hole they were in.

Things finally started to turn around by mid-2005. Milestone adopted a new business model where they completed more residential service jobs. They were no longer at the mercy of contractors and could stop doing construction jobs. They ditched the U-Haul business and focused entirely on the trade. They got two technicians on the road with dedicated trucks. Each technician brought in $4,000 to $5,000 a week, and they booked five to seven calls a day. They finally started to put money into the bank, which was life-changing. Best of all, three months after the start of her illness, Sabrina fully recovered, and Mark was able to return to Milestone full time.

With guidance from SGI, word was spreading about Milestone's customer-focused business, and service requests were coming in faster than they could get technicians out on the road. They needed another truck, but there were some obstacles in the way. After the SGI investment, Gus and Mark couldn't afford a truck at market value. This was ironic because they needed another truck to take on more business and pay off the existing loans. They had no credit for financing and couldn't take out another loan. At this time, Milestone had three trucks and one had just been repossessed because they couldn't afford to pay it off.

They had no choice but to locate a tote-the-note auto sale shop. The auto shop they selected was known for advertising they'd take "good credit, bad credit, or no credit at all." As Gus and Mark perused the inventory, they stumbled upon a van that could work. It already had four hundred thousand miles on it. The salesman offered a "drive off the lot" sale price at $4,800. But Gus and Mark didn't have it. Not even close.

"All right, how about no down payment and twelve payments of $800, and we have a deal?" the salesman offered.

Twelve payments of $800 a month meant $9,600 in a year. It was double the price, but the deal meant they could have the van that day. Plus, the monthly payment was a lot easier to swing than the full payment.

They thought it over and decided that, despite being a horrible deal, it was better than nothing. They bought the van and kept it in the field for six years. Throughout the van's life as a service vehicle, Milestone spent at least $25,000 on repairs to keep it running.

First Milestone-branded van

Life at Milestone was beyond stressful. There were not enough technicians on the road to meet the demand of customers. Gus and Mark were still tweaking their business model and organizing accounts. Milestone was growing but slowly. Keeping the doors open was a gargantuan task, but over time, that little van produced almost $4 million in revenue for Milestone. It is affectionally nicknamed the "Rainbow Truck" for the large blue, yellow, and red stripes emblazoned on the side. It was the first vehicle to don Milestone's multicolored logo. Today, that truck sits in one of the Milestone office buildings and serves as a reminder of humble beginnings and how far the company has come.

As Gus and Mark paid the monthly payments on the old truck, they continued to grow the business. Not wanting to make another desperate vehicle purchase, they searched for other options. To finance a new vehicle, they would need at least $50,000 up front and would have to pay another $20,000 to wrap it with the Milestone logo and colors and outfit it with equipment. At that point, $70,000 was more than the entire quarterly profit and would be impossible without a loan. Gus and Mark talked to every bank in the Dallas–Fort Worth area, but with the current state of operations, no one would extend them the credit they needed.

They prayed and continued business as usual until one day Gus received a postcard with a huge heart on its front. Written on the heart were the words "We Love Contractors." He flipped it over and found the contact information for a man named David of First Bank of Canyon Creek. Gus gave him a call.

"Hi, David. This is Gus from Milestone Electric. I got a postcard for your bank in the mail. We're in need of an honest bank that would be willing to work with us. The banks I've been to have all refused us services."

"I'll come to your office for a meeting," David said.

A few days later, David arrived wearing a suit and tie. His collar was crisp, and his black shoes were polished. He was very conservative with his words, and Gus and Mark never could tell what he was thinking or if he was going to say anything at all. They gave him a tour of the building and wondered if he thought it was the worst thing or the best thing he'd seen all week. After the tour, the trio retreated to Mark's office. David spent nearly two hours asking every smart question imaginable. He wanted to know about the current debt, cashflow, average number of service orders per month and per year, and where Gus and Mark saw Milestone in five and ten years. At that point, they half expected David to say, "give me a call in a few years when you have a longer credit history." As the meeting came to a close, David made his decision.

"I don't think I told you, but I'm actually president of the bank. I'll help you guys. You're doing honest work and running your company right. Send us what you need, and we'll get it done for you."

For the first time in Milestone's journey, a banker saw past the dollars and debt. Milestone would finally be able to borrow money and get some assets. Gus and Mark banked with David for the next five years until he sold the bank and went to another. To this day, David remains a huge friend of Milestone.

In business, you're always scared, always on the edge, always pushing the envelope. When you're in that space, you're in the right place because you're walking the path of faith. Despite every closed door, Gus and Mark never lost faith.

Finally, Milestone was becoming what Gus and Mark wanted the business to be all along—a service to others. Milestone's purpose was clear, and its values would develop as Milestone grew.

Walter Byxbe
Shane Shipley Dan Tullos Josh
Carter Mark Roberts Whitney Reynolds
Joe Camacho Ty Godwin Jason Martin Adel Solis
David Davis Randall Johnston David Chandler Kirk Grace
Tammy Lund Candace Prather James Hicks Don Hoel Paul Ford
Glenn Bland Jason Bailey Sam Stratton Dustin Bramlett Jimmy May-
field Thomas Wilson Ireta Drane Mellisa Holland John Durr Michael
Leasure Jake Brown Chase Palmer Shane Healy Debbie Tucker John Trimble
Rob Crowson Scott Allison Jeni Gant Luke Strange David Goodin Steven
Tigert Trey Calhoun Shane Healy   John Taylor Kristofor Wildes Brad
Wilson Jennifer Guenther Jesse   Andrade Kirk Browder Antho-
ny Gutteres Matthew Holton   Crystal Butterfield Stephen
Waldrep Justin Buttrill Chris   Perkins Steven Overton Rodney
                                       Rasmussen Chris Hughes Scott
                                       Johnston Corrina Piel Chris
                                       Pollard Adam Jones Nathan
                                       Ellis Zaaron Mitchel Casey Sells
                                       Ashley Wilkinson Lauren Kinney
                                       Pamela Smith Heather Roddy
                                       Jennifer Williams Missy Jones
                                       Joe Decaria Jacob Henderson
                                       Greg Capote Deon Thompson
                                       Kenneth Marshall David
                                       Downs Chris Grant Gary
                                       Ryan Aaron Mitchell Todd   Parker Paul Ford Jason
Oesch Charles Cortinaz Kevin Martinez Cody Paschall Tillie
Pinson Tommy Allen Stephen Waldrep John Vavra Travis Mount
Daniel Ruiz Dalton Brewer John Vavra Gustavo Aguirre Patricia Hunter
Jimmy McManus Colin Stacy Roger Marsh Austin Porter Alex Clumpner
Tyler Shirley Loren Guay Kerry Malsam Lawrence Carter Heather Mayfield
Brandon Kearney Tracy Moreland Chris Kohr Craig Morris Matt Hall Christian
Soberanes Jeffrey Roberson Robert Shier Hailee Goellner Chris Brian Christopher
Sanchez Chris Hines Wayne Worthen Jason Adams Taylor Pritchett Michael Raymond

SERVING YOUR PURPOSE AND VALUES

Whatever you do, work at it with all your heart.

—*Colossians 3:23 NIV*

"I may not always agree with what you guys believe, but I have never been treated better by another company," a team member told Gus one day after a brief discussion on values. Gus saw this as the highest of compliments, a testament to Milestone's values, purpose, and core identity.

At Milestone, everything each team member does is to serve a higher purpose. Milestone strives to be the most impactful company in the Dallas–Fort Worth area. As the company grew, Mark, Gus, and their team came together to solidify what Milestone stands for: to enrich everyone who works here, every customer, and every member of the community. To put it plainly, Milestone exists to make other people's lives better. That knowledge, and every decision the company makes, comes from faith. Running Milestone according to their faith came naturally because that's really how Milestone came to be.

From the very first day, the Milestone team strived to be intentional about sharing Milestone's values of Faith, Family, and Excellence through the actions they take and the words they say. On top of that, they believe if you hire people who embody the same values as the company, then the values of your organization shine through. At the end of the day, corporations don't have values. People do.

Faith

Milestone is a faith-based company. It was founded by faith and is run by the faith of their leadership. Gus and Mark had faith from the get-go, so it is no surprise this is a key Milestone value. Faith is trusting that there is a bigger purpose and a larger perspective beyond what you can see at the moment. When a team member hosts a meeting, they often begin with a prayer for wisdom. The Bible challenges all of us to "hunger and thirst for righteousness" (Matthew 5:6 NIV) and desire wisdom above riches and gold (Proverbs 8:11 and 16:6 NIV). Wisdom is trying to figure out what makes things work and why things are the way they are, so the team asks God for support in that pursuit.

If someone doesn't share in a Christian-based faith, Gus, Mark, or anyone at Milestone certainly doesn't force their participation or ostracize them in any way. Fortunately, the company's core values are shared across many faiths, allowing for wider participation. However, the team will not stop praying simply because someone on the team has different beliefs.

Milestone believes in the golden rule to "treat others the way you wish to be treated." Then, do things well and honestly and, finally, be a good steward of what you have. These are principles everyone can get behind, whether they are faith-minded or not. Faith serves as the basis for how decisions are made within the company, and Milestone is a vehicle to reach people. Milestone brings people together and creates an ecosystem that makes everyone's lives better through faith and living these values.

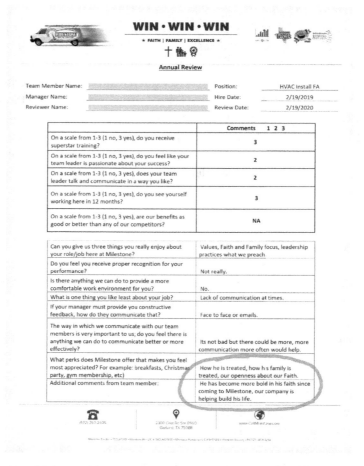

Annual Culture and Care review: team member testimony revealing the profound positive effects the Milestone culture has had on the team member and his family

Family

The second Milestone value is Family. This value of Family is probably different than what people may think. To the Milestone team, family means responsibility, because everyone should be accountable to one another. And family doesn't just encompass the people in one's personal life.

If a technician is on a call and running late to his next appointment, another one will stop over in their free time to help because that is what one would do for a friend or family member. If someone in the office is way behind on their work and trying to get out at a decent hour to get home to their family, someone else always pitches in to help because that is how a family supports each other. If someone needs to go on vacation or if something happens to someone's spouse, everyone picks up the slack for the affected person without being told to.

When Milestone team member Scott's wife took ill, he didn't want to sit at home alone while she was in the hospital. Scott was with his wife as often as possible, but he didn't want the free time to be alone with his thoughts. He wanted to be with his family, his Milestone family. Scott came to work because he felt loved and supported. He knew he could talk to his fellow team members. Team members took turns visiting Scott's wife until she recovered. That is what family is all about.

When something happens to one member of Milestone, it happens to every member of Milestone. If you talk to team members and ask them what Milestone is, they will tell you it is a big family. When you dissect why they feel like that, it is because they know every single person cares about them. This love and care even extends to team members' spouses. Each month, Milestone hosts a company-wide breakfast and encourages everyone to bring their spouses to the event. Milestone even sends satisfaction surveys to team members' spouses, asking them how their partners' employment has impacted their lives. This family relationship is what keeps Milestone team members dedicated and united for a common purpose.

Father and son at Milestone family meeting

Excellence

The third value, Excellence, simply refers to doing the little things right every single time. An example Gus and Mark like to use to define this value is interesting. Think about how members of the military make their beds. Each morning, they meticulously fold their sheets and neatly arrange their bed to prepare for inspection. In the military, you're taught to make your bed with precision. The thought behind this is, if you make your bed right, that is one excellent thing you did that day. Everything builds on that one thing—you start your day with excellence and keep it going through everything you do. This is how the Milestone team approaches their work.

All technicians wear white starched shirts, ironed pants, and shined shoes. Everyone is well groomed and looks their best. Ideally, each vehicle is always spotless inside and out. The tools are clean, functional, and tested frequently. This is a testament to the pride technicians feel regarding their work and their tools of the trade. Most often, the offices are organized and meticulous. When you do everything with excellence, you produce excellent results. Excellence is not a skill; it is an attitude.

That all might sound like a lot, but in practice, it's just conducting business the way you conduct your life outside of work. Values aren't something you create. They're who you are. Your company's values will either be something you have intentionally shared or unintentionally revealed. S. Truett Cathy (founder of Chick-fil-A) said it best: "No amount of business school training or work experience can teach what is ultimately a matter of personal character. Businesses are not dishonest or greedy. People are. Thus, a business, successful or not, is merely a reflection of the character of its leadership."[1]

Milestone is intentional about everything. The team members see themselves as stewards over the company instead of simply employees. Regardless of successes, Milestone doesn't exist to profit; Milestone profits to exist.

---

1 Quoted in Don McKee, "Believing It's Easier to Succeed Than to Fail Food for Thought," Cherokee Tribune & Ledger-News, April 27, 2016, https://www.tribuneledgernews .com/ledger/believing-it-s-easier-to-succeed-than-to-fail-food/article_4e87315a-0bfb -11e6-9191-c39649e02850.html.

At the end of the day, people don't want just a job like their parents had. They want to feel like there's a purpose to what they're doing. They want meaningful work. Milestone is all about connecting people and making them feel like they are a part of something special.

Annual Halloween Costume Contest at Milestone

Milestone's Annual Holiday Party is always a hit!

Tony Broyles
Valerie Stevens Dominic Stop-
piello Ryan Cox Jason Wright Joshua Harris
Jonathan Phillips Chris Villarreal Chris Villegas Manuel
Vasquez Nick Kirby Kira Beaver Valerie Stevens Stacy Love
Chris Salinas Keith Hernandez Ray Gonzales William Witty Ste-
phen Stone David Matheny Jay Thompson Eric Ballard Marco Sierra
Christopher Smith Shawn Dunn Michael Sweeney Robert Nickerson John
Darisse Myles Humphrey Toriano King Daniel Grimes Nick Nabors
James Bledsoe Steven Belcher Anthony McCoy Martin Gerlets
Casey Wilson Bryan Tenan Chris Wingo David Crites Judson
Dozier Ryan LaFountain Christo-
pher Brown Nathan Sparkman
William Whitton Orlando Lopez
Brian Dunn Amaury Barreda Jacob
Thompson Margaret Hoover
Gary Wright Jeff Robertson
Taneishia Dugger Lucas Mazyck
Shelley Edwards Megan Tidwell Byron
Byars April Smith Zachary Wood Bradley
Williamson Dustin Owens Jessi
Bratcher Don Pearce Michael
Dark Dayn Barrett Carl Thomas
Patricia Eskridge Arthur Gooch Ashley Nickerson Chris Mal-
has Donald Jamison III Michael Reynolds-White Carlos Flores
Jorge Leon Guillermo Ruiz Ge- rardo Garcia Lorraine Widmer
Mike Stevens Dusty Whitley Alan Tuttle Gary Garcia Brian Ashley
David Flores Loy Towse Chris Killikelly Kevin Torti Krystal McGee Josh Forson
Jeff Arnold Michael Whitten Rebecca Campos Randy Whitten Tony Sharpton
Mannie Owings Mike Stoll DeVonte' Davenport Richard Baker Brandon
Rainbolt Ricky Golden Lee Spencer Patrick Riland Peter Smith Matt
Heisserman Josh McKenzie Chris Kirkham Leonardo Villarreal
Eric Kleiber Austin Geist Rebecca Gerber Kevin Sandefer
Dylan Freeman Michael Payne Misael
Salazar Lira

RIDING FOR THE BRAND

As iron sharpens iron, so one person sharpens another.

—Proverbs 27:17 NIV

In his book *The Ideal Team Player: How to Recognize and Cultivate the Three Essential Virtues*, Patrick Lencionci shares three indispensable virtues that make teams successful.[2] These virtues are humble, hungry, and smart. A humble team member focuses on others more than on themselves. They are willing to help others have the best idea and for others to get a share of the credit for success. Humble people are respectful people. A hungry team member has a tremendously strong work ethic and strives for excellence. Hungry people want to grow and succeed. They take care of themselves and the people around them. If you think about the structure of family throughout history, the man would go out and make sure the family was fed. He had to be hungry. He couldn't be lazy. He had the motivation to take care of his loved ones. Finally, a smart team member doesn't necessarily mean intellectually smart but rather emotionally intelligent. Smart team members are emotionally aware of those around them. They know how their words and actions impact others and are compassionate and intuitive.

Milestone continuously searches for people who are humble, hungry, and smart, and who align with the core values of Faith, Family, and Excellence. To accomplish this, the human resources team, which is called the Culture and Care team, deploys a meticulous hiring process. Many people call in to Milestone asking for a job. About three out of ten individuals who are interviewed are offered a position. The average cost to bring a new team member on in any industry is higher than keeping the people you have. Therefore, Milestone invests just as much in hiring as in marketing and sales.

Before a prospective team member is offered an interview, they must complete a comprehensive aptitude test related to their field of choice. These tests measure the candidate's level of "humble, hungry, and smart." The Culture and Care team make this screening process as scientific as possible to ensure the candidate will be someone who will ride for the brand.

---

2 Patrick Lencionci, *The Ideal Team Player: How to Recognize and Cultivate the Three Essential Virtues* (Hoboken, NJ: John Wiley & Sons, 2016).

Riding for the brand means you must be someone who will represent Milestone on and off the job. Who are you on the weekends? If you practice Milestone's values in your daily life outside the job, you are riding for the brand. You "bleed" red and yellow, Milestone's colors.

When a prospective team member comes for their interview, they get a warm welcome when they walk in the door. Let's say there is a prospective candidate named Timothy. When he arrives for his interview, he'll see a big monitor behind the front desk that reads, "Timothy, Welcome to Milestone. We are glad you are here."

During his interview, Timothy will receive a comprehensive tour of the facility. He'll meet various team members. The goal is for him to feel welcomed and wanted. Almost immediately after the interview, a team member follows up with a phone call or text message thanking the prospect for coming in and spending time with the Milestone family. Timothy will receive a handwritten note with everyone's signature, even if an offer is not extended. At the end of the day, the goal is to offer the candidate a positive experience, no matter what.

If Timothy is a good fit and he accepts the job offer, a new level of hospitality is delivered on his first day. Milestone wants new team members to feel like they're joining a family, not just starting a new chapter in their lives. Timothy will meet every single person in the office. At the conclusion of onboarding, the entire team will gather together and present Timothy with a special welcome basket filled with candy, books, and a big blanket, with *Faith*, *Family*, and *Excellence* embroidered on the fabric. If Timothy is married, he'll be given a small gift from Milestone for his spouse. If he has children, he'll receive additional gifts, including a Bible with his kid's names on it and a note that reads, "This book helped us a lot in life, and we hope it helps you too."

When a new team member joins the Milestone family, important information such as their birthday, their spouses' and children's birthdays, and their anniversary are recorded. On those dates, a card signed by the whole team and a gift card are mailed to the team member's house. The truth is, when an individual joins a company, his or her whole family joins. That decision affects each of their lives.

New team members get to know each other with fun introduction games

Milestone is very passionate about refining the hiring process because each team member knows you only have one life to live. The sooner you find your family or home, the better you and everyone connected with you will be, even if that home is not Milestone. One of the things Milestone does to check on the newest family members is a ninety-day review. Milestone's Culture and Care team conducts a review (the new team member will be more open with someone other than their direct team leader), asking questions such as "Do you enjoy working here?" "Does the job meet your expectations?" "Do you know what our values are?" "Do you see yourself working here in a year?"

People don't quit jobs; they quit bosses. This ninety-day check-in is one way to evaluate the happiness of new team members. Milestone creates an environment where people flourish. When you connect with like-minded people who understand and support your mission and values, your business will flourish. As an employee, you spend more time with people at work than you do at home. You want to hire people you wouldn't mind spending a four-hour layover at an airport with. In short, you want to enjoy the people you work with.

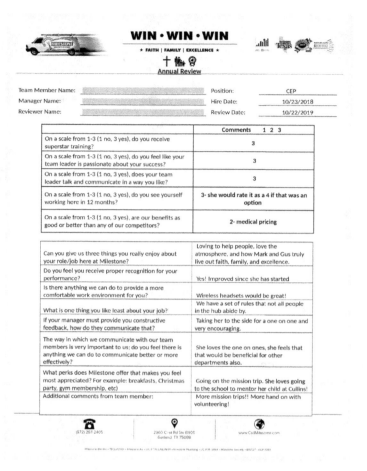

WIN · WIN · WIN
★ FAITH | FAMILY | EXCELLENCE ★

✝ 👪 🌐

__Annual Review__

Team Member Name:		Position:	CEP
Manager Name:		Hire Date:	10/23/2018
Reviewer Name:		Review Date:	10/22/2019

	Comments 1 2 3
On a scale from 1-3 (1 no, 3 yes), do you receive superstar training?	3
On a scale from 1-3 (1 no, 3 yes), do you feel like your team leader is passionate about your success?	3
On a scale from 1-3 (1 no, 3 yes), does your team leader talk and communicate in a way you like?	3
On a scale from 1-3 (1 no, 3 yes), do you see yourself working here in 12 months?	3- she would rate it as a 4 if that was an option
On a scale from 1-3 (1 no, 3 yes), are our benefits as good or better than any of our competitors?	2- medical pricing

Can you give us three things you really enjoy about your role/job here at Milestone?	Loving to help people, love the atmosphere, and how Mark and Gus truly live out faith, family, and excellence.
Do you feel you receive proper recognition for your performance?	Yes! Improved since she has started
Is there anything we can do to provide a more comfortable work environment for you?	Wireless headsets would be great!
What is one thing you like least about your job?	We have a set of rules that not all people in the hub abide by.
If your manager must provide you constructive feedback, how do they communicate that?	Taking her to the side for a one on one and very encouraging.
The way in which we communicate with our team members is very important to us; do you feel there is anything we can do to communicate better or more effectively?	She loves the one on ones, she feels that that would be beneficial for other departments also.
What perks does Milestone offer that makes you feel most appreciated? For example: breakfasts, Christmas party, gym membership, etc)	Going on the mission trip. She loves going to the school to mentor her child at Cullins!
Additional comments from team member:	More mission trips!! More hand on with volunteering!

☎ (972) 287-2405   📍 2360 C st Rd Sw B900 Garland, TX 75088   🌐 www.CallMilestone.com

Team member annual review

People cross paths every day. If you pay close attention, those people may have crossed your path for a reason. Gus and Mark discovered that early on, when a series of events led them to hire individuals who would grow with Milestone and demonstrate exactly what it means to ride for the brand.

Once Milestone Electric was up and running, Gus and Mark got involved as mentors in a youth program at their church. One afternoon, as the youth group wrapped for the day, a young man named Eric approached them.

"Hi, I'm looking for some work for the summer. Would you guys have a part-time job or something I could apply for?" Eric asked.

This was around the time when Gus and Mark had limited financial and material resources. They didn't have any openings that sixteen-year-old Eric would qualify for, but they saw that moment as an opportunity to do something good.

A few days later, Gus and Mark combined a few odd jobs around the office and brought Eric on board. He did anything and everything, including cleaning up after the pest control cats that caught the rats around the office. Eric vacuumed the office, helped with paperwork, took out the trash—you'd name it, he'd do it. Gus and Mark recognized that Eric would do absolutely anything to be a part of the team.

Eric worked for Milestone through high school. After his senior year, he left and went to college. He worked his butt off but decided college just wasn't the right fit for him. Eric was hungry for work. He wanted to learn by trade, not in the classroom. After two years, he returned to the Milestone family.

Fresh off the college circuit, Eric began administrative work. He answered phones, completed basic accounting tasks, and entered paperwork into the Milestone computer system. That was a little over ten years ago. Since then, Eric has served as a data entry specialist, payroll manager, and accounting manager, and now he supervises three team leaders over accounting, Culture and Care, and recruiting. Eric meets weekly with his team, and they are always excited and interested in their jobs.

One thing Gus and Mark learned is that sometimes you have to meet people where they are. They learned that lesson by what happened with Stuart.

One afternoon, one of the team members noticed a young man digging in one of the dumpsters outside. He wasn't bothering anyone, but it was clear he was living a rough life, and the guys at Milestone knew he needed some help.

Without hesitation, Gus and Mark decided they would do whatever it took to help the young man and decided to hire him.

The next day they went back out to the dumpsters looking for the young man, and sure enough, they found him.

"Stuart, I bet you're a good kid. How would you like to work here at Milestone?"

"What would I do?" he asked, a wave of disbelief permeating his voice.

"Well, we'd get you trained, and you could start as an apprentice. Part of working here is looking presentable. We can help with that."

"But one of the other conditions of working here is you'll need to pass a drug test. We'll test monthly, and if you fail, that is it. You're out."

Stuart paused for a minute, unsure how to respond. He knew this was an opportunity he shouldn't pass up.

"I don't know what I did to deserve this, but I'll do it. I won't let you down," Stuart replied.

After meeting with Gus, Stuart received his uniform and apprentice training. Immediately, he took pride in his work and himself. It was the second chance he never knew he needed.

Stuart became one of Milestone's top electricians. Stuart sold and installed more equipment than any other technician. The company has received reviews from customers saying, "Stuart is the only technician I trust with my home." If an apprentice needs guidance, Stuart is the go-to. He not only believes in Milestone's values of Faith, Family, and Excellence, but he lives them each and every day.

New team members' first day at Milestone team building during Culture Day

From: John Mendoza
Sent: Saturday, November 2, 2019 11:05 AM
To: Mark Caldwell; Constantine "Gus" Antos; Mark Robison; Joe DeCaria; Ireta Drane
Subject: Box of Bibles

Not that I needed any more confirmation that the Lord had me right where I needed to be in my career, but the box of Bibles we received this morning completely overwhelmed my family and me. I mean, seriously, there is no other company in any kind of profession that is this invested in their employees. It's unheard of to do the things that y'all do on a daily basis to take care of us, and it does not go unnoticed. I can't express enough how thankful I am to work with Milestone. Thanks to each of you for all you do to keep this company biblical and living out the gospel in your lives.

New team member's email after receiving welcome gift in mail

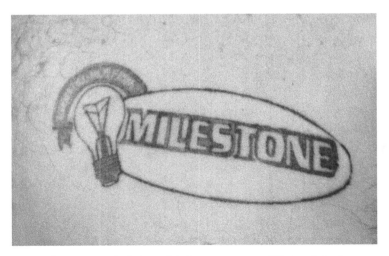

One team member's show of dedication—an ACTUAL Milestone tattoo!

When blessed with the opportunity to make a difference, Milestone will seize that opportunity, yet sometimes God sends people to Milestone when Gus and Mark least expect it. One day, a man named Humberto walked into the shop. He told Gus he lived a few blocks away and was looking for work.

"I need a job," he told Gus. "I would do anything you need."

At the time, Gus and Mark had just decided to change the Milestone vehicle wraps. There were three trucks that needed the old wraps removed so the new ones could be installed. It was perfect timing. They told Humberto they didn't have a long-term position, but he could work on the vehicle wraps and get paid by the day. It took Humberto three days to complete the job, and after that, he asked if anything else needed to be done.

"Okay, well, why don't you help us clean up the shop?" Gus suggested.

Humberto humbly agreed. He just wanted to work. Everyone was impressed by his good attitude and work ethic. He treated everyone with respect and completed every job with excellence.

Although an exciting opportunity was not available, Gus and Mark eventually hired Humberto full time. All these years later, Humberto is still with Milestone and is always smiling. Now Milestone has four different facilities, and Humberto manages them all. He does an exceptional job and has continued to grow with Milestone. His wife joined the team about five years ago, helping keep the offices in order.

To honor everything Humberto represents, Gus and Mark named an award after him. Each year, they pick a team member who gives the best of themselves without expecting anything in return and does so with an amazing sense of hospitality and grace, just like Humberto. They've been giving out the Humberto Award for about ten years now. Humberto embodies what the people of Milestone are all about. Like Eric and Stuart, Humberto was humble, hungry, and smart.

If Milestone's purpose is to make people's lives better, both customers and team members, then the right people who fit in the organization are essential. It is serendipitous when those people find Milestone, but the company also puts in a lot of intentional effort to find them. When core values are values embraced by people, that is, values lived out in daily life, and team members feel like they're a part of something bigger, it is a Win-Win-Win.

Noel Ochoa Stacy Hale Aven Polk Sarah
Kirk Charles Sage Mark Bransom Jeremy
Eastham Colton Mosley Buturm Peoples
Tim Edwards Justin Lockridge Justin Holland
Stephen King Jana Edwards Gene Roberts
Joshua Bomardelli John Vayo Joel Hamnes Dar-
rell Wilson Justin Robison Joe Gomez Casey Gann
Steve Squires Paul Wallace Chad Strickland Dustin
Martin Colby Murphy Hunter Nickell Julio Gutierrez
Skyler Keatts Francisco Gutierrez Shayde Wood Joshua
Pennington Juana Guevara Stephan Turner Jose Padilla
Judy Campbell Richard Davis   Willaim Loudermilk Jim Bell
Crystal Bruce Leah Delong   Garrett Harris Anthony Ste-
phens Steven Laliberte Ar-   turo Moreno Adam Lotspeich
Tammy Terrill Kristyn Beau-   champ Francisco Hernandez
Adam Stahr Ray Washington   Jennifer Tutt Grant Hunter
Tyler Nelson Tommy Tang   Madison Vrbnjak Austin Tenan
Ashlie Payne Jerry Slagel   Elizabeth Brenden Philip King
Johnathan White Devon   Reynolds Natalee Weber Luke
Chambliss Ciara Bogle Courtney Jones David Whitton Lou Sizemore Tomas Soto Ste-
phen Schultz Zachary Garcia Sandra Dickson Zachary Davis Christopher Warn Alfredo
Vasquez Michael Alexander Phillip Blake Oliver Roque Jarrod Tawney Omar Villalobos
Favian Silva Jason Thompson Timothy Thresher Juan Herrera Aaron Pattee Charles
Castillo Edwin Ochoa Jarod Tucker Brandon Menzies JoAnna Tawney Jack Barnett
Dillon Ashton Nick Norville Bryan Rauscher Jordan Bauer Guillermo Mena William Pier-
son Tyler Dooley Jonathan Jackson Riley Dobbe Trystan Sellers Adam Farmer Braeden
Hughes Moshe Kramer Sebastian Ramirez Briana Nunez Cameron Carroccia Justin
Kilgore Kiara "KC" Carras-
co Joel Garcia Jennifer Gip-
son Shawnee Morris Kelby
Beasley Jessica Nottingham
Morgan Montgomery Se-
quoia Malone Chayne Baxley

WIN-WIN-WIN

**Each of you should use whatever gift
you have received to serve others,
as faithful stewards of God's
grace in its various forms.**

—1 Peter 4:10 NIV

Milestone was growing, and it was time for a bigger (and rodent-free) location. When Gus and Mark moved Milestone to a new office in 2006, they installed a floor-to-ceiling-sized yellow-and-blue three-dimensional sign in one of the main hallways. The larger-than-life reminder is Milestone's mantra: Win-Win-Win.

Milestone campus walls emphasize the Win-Win-Win mindset!

If Milestone's mission was to be the most impactful company in their community, then Win-Win-Win would be the strategy to reach that mission. Around 2005, Gus and Mark saw a company on the East Coast whose mission was "We want our team to win, our customers to win, and our company to win."[3] It caught their attention in a big way. They both knew it was the perfect fit for Milestone.

If the team wins, the customer wins, and if the customer wins, ultimately the company wins. However, to Mark and Gus, their team is the number one priority. For the team to have a solid foundation to care for customers, they too have to feel supported and understood.

As the business was growing, many Milestone customers started to request service on Saturdays and Sundays. As a premier residential services provider, the Milestone team answered the call of duty and

---

3 "Milestone Electric: Service Contractors of the Year," Independent Electrical Contractors, https://www.ieci.org/newsroom-and-insights /milestone-electric-service-contractors-of-the-year.

accommodated those customers as well as they could. It wasn't easy. At the time, team leaders scheduled technicians for jobs. If they sent a technician out on a Saturday or Sunday, they would give that technician Monday and Tuesday off. The problem was managers couldn't be scheduled the same way because there were so few of them. It usually came down to one guy managing an entire department. While his technicians could shuffle around their schedules to get a day off here and there, the manager would end up working seven days a week to support the weekend load.

For the team to win, Gus and Mark had to do something. Managers were burning out, and their job was taking them away from their families. The leadership team got together and developed a process for an "emergency fee." If a customer wanted service completed on a Saturday or Sunday, they'd be subject to an additional fee. This option worked to reduce the demand, but they still had some interesting requests for weekend jobs. One time, a customer called and requested weekend service for a ceiling fan installation, which is not exactly an emergency. The customer offered to pay the fee because they *really* wanted that ceiling fan installed. To protect the interests of the technicians and managers, Milestone declined the service and rescheduled it for a weekday.

Some people might call that turning down revenue. Serving that customer would have helped the customer and would have helped the company. But would it have helped the team? No. Therefore, it was not a true Win-Win-Win. If one "win" is missing, the whole system is broken.

When making a decision, the team tries to stop and ask, "Is this a Win-Win-Win?" If it is not, like the situation above, the team works to find a way where everyone wins. This idea guides all team members to make informed decisions about their work.

Breakfast Time: Team Wins

Throughout its growth, Gus, Mark, and the Milestone team have been dedicated to enriching the lives of team members. Some of this enrichment happened by accident. Back in mid-2004, Gus and Mark held a "family meeting" at Grandy's restaurant in Rockwall, Texas. They invited two technicians and one of their office team members, their entire team at the time. The five of them huddled around a tiny table near the front window. Gus and Mark used their time together to learn what was going on in their team members' lives. It was an informal way to check in with them. The breakfast went well, so they started having them once a week. It was a great way to start the day, and the informal check-in made the team feel more connected. Eventually more team members joined the informal gathering.

"Why don't we invite our team members' spouses to join us for a family breakfast?" Gus asked Mark one day. Mark agreed it was a good idea, and they started opening the weekly gatherings to spouses as well. As the team grew, Gus and Mark pulled back and started hosting them once a month instead of once a week. The interest grew to the point where they could no longer fit everyone at Grandy's. They had to rent out a local hotel meeting room!

The breakfast evolved in many ways. First, Gus and Mark shared some company updates. Then they would bring in a guest speaker—someone notable who shared the Milestone message and values or had something inspiring to share with the Milestone family. Afterward, they would hand out awards, like the Humberto Award, to outstanding team members who had recently gone above and beyond expectations. There have been some memorable family breakfasts over the years.

Site of first family meeting. Current family meetings are held at an event center to accommodate five hundred-plus guests!

One morning in 2011, Gus was excited to share some really big news.

"Mark, I've got good news. Roger Staubach is coming to our next family breakfast," Gus said with a grin.

"You've got to be kidding me," Mark replied in disbelief.

Gus laughed and glanced around at the Dallas Cowboys memorabilia Mark had displayed throughout his office. Gus knew having Roger Staubach attend the company's family breakfast was a big deal for Milestone and Mark. They got lucky. Staubach is not only an NFL MVP, but he is also an influential faith-based individual within the Dallas–Fort Worth community. He was exactly the kind of guest speaker who could make an impact on the Milestone family.

Everyone was excited for that breakfast, especially Mark. Staubach was one of Mark's childhood heroes. Mark spent much of his formative years watching Staubach on the field. During the visit, Staubach even signed a few pieces of Mark's favorite Cowboys' gear. It was a special thing to witness.

For other breakfasts, Milestone has welcomed members of the military to come in and share their stories of inspiration. One such notable guest was Lieutenant Clay Spicer, a member of the First Cavalry Division that came under surprise attack in Sadr City, Iraq, on April 4, 2004, a day now known as "Black Sunday." At another breakfast, Milestone hosted retired Navy captain and author of *Turn This Ship Around: A True Story of Turning Followers into Leaders*, David Marquet, who shared stories of leadership and challenge. Today, nearly five hundred team members and spouses attend the family breakfast.

Milestone Family Breakfast now held in a hotel ballroom or event facility to accommodate the group's size!

A Little Something Extra: The Customer Wins

When the team wins, the customer wins. The deliberate measures taken to ensure team member satisfaction trickle right down to each and every customer. Every job comes with a 100 percent satisfaction guarantee. If the customer is even the tiniest bit dissatisfied with Milestone's work, they will receive a full refund. Mark and Gus knew this was a risky move as people could abuse the guarantee, but they trusted their customers. If customers had faith Milestone would do the best job possible, Mark and Gus knew the team would deliver. It was easy to back a decision everyone on the team believed in.

Beyond completing quality work, Milestone technicians enjoy delivering simple but special perks to their customers. If a customer has children, technicians will arrive at the home equipped with a ten-page coloring book featuring Milestone Mark battling a surge protector monster. Have a dog? Technicians carry a supply of dog treats with them for customers' pets. Milestone recently ran a hilarious commercial featuring a dog causing all sorts of HVAC and plumbing mayhem, so Milestone would come out to service the home and bring dog treats. These are just small ways of saying, "we care about your family."

To make an impact and strengthen the customer relationship, technicians also look for ways they can complete an extra task for a customer. Gus and Mark felt that a little unexpected value could go a long way—not just for the customer but also for the technician. Both parties leave the service call feeling good. It provides for a memorable experience.

Milestone customers always get the red-carpet treatment!

Let's say a technician conducts (pun intended) a wiring job. While there, they'll keep their eyes open for a small task they can complete. It could be moving a washing machine so it stops rattling, applying oil to a squeaky door, even starting a car that was giving a customer trouble. These tasks are beyond their scope of work but demonstrate Milestone's commitment to making customers' lives better.

During every visit, technicians are encouraged to change light bulbs in hard-to-reach places, put fresh batteries in smoke detectors, and, for elderly customers, find something heavy that needs to be moved or carried. It is like a scavenger hunt for "good deeds."

When technicians do this, the customer loses sight of the cost of the service. They feel like they've received more than 100 percent value. Today, it is becoming harder to find companies in the American service industry who still deliver that kind of experience.

Milestone even has policies written around this. All technicians wear shoe protectors in customers' homes to avoid tracking in mud or dirt.

They utilize tool carpets—pads they lay under their tools—to protect hardwood floors from scratches or dings the heavy tools could cause. Customers are emailed a short video featuring their expected technician. This allows the customer to feel comfortable letting the Milestone team member into their home.

This attitude is so deeply ingrained in the Milestone culture that it is practiced outside the customers' homes on a regular basis. Technicians have stumbled upon stranded drivers on the way to a service call and pulled over to help the stranger in need. They've blocked traffic after car accidents to ensure a clear path for emergency responders.

On one memorable occasion, a technician was heading back to the shop when he noticed a car pulled off to the side of the road with smoke billowing from the hood. He thought the car might be overheating, but after rolling the window down, he could smell burning plastic and oil.

Without hesitation, he pulled a safe distance behind the vehicle. Upon approaching the car, he saw flames. He ran to the driver's side and found a woman with her children in the backseat stuck inside the car. Her seatbelt was jammed. Quickly he cut the belt and rescued the family, moving them far away from the inferno. When Mark and Gus heard what happened, they shared the story with the entire Milestone family. That selfless act is still talked about today.

Milestone has created a culture where technicians think, "How can I make a difference in someone's life today?" There are two hundred beacons of light going out into the metroplex every single day, each equipped to go into a customer's home, take care of problems, and do something nice for them. Or they can do something nice for a complete stranger they meet along the way. That is a lot of impact.

Striving for Impact: Everyone Wins

We've learned that if our team is made up of like-minded people with the same values, then, ultimately, they want to do good things! In 2016, a member of the Culture and Care team spotted a JetBlue Christmas commercial where passengers told a computer what they wanted for Christmas before boarding their flight. After these special passengers landed, their wish-list gifts arrived on the luggage claim. The gesture was spot-on with the spirit of Christmas. As the commercial continued to air, more Milestone team members saw it. Soon, everyone was thinking the same thing. They wanted to pull off a similar feat and just "bless people for no reason."

Travis and the marketing team got to work. They created survey cards about Milestone services with a fun question at the bottom: "What is one thing you would like for Christmas this year?" The customers thought it was a routine quality-and-control effort with a holiday twist. They sent their cards back, and Milestone began planning an epic Christmas surprise.

The team broke up into groups and went to Best Buy, Walmart, toy stores, and sporting goods shops to purchase the wish-list items. They bought doll houses, Maroon 5 tickets, trips to Las Vegas, and even a two-week cruise. The company spent over $15,000 on the items and hand-delivered the gifts to their very surprised customers (and caught the whole thing on film). New team members joined forces with veteran team members to support the initiative. It was a Christmas the community and Milestone would never forget.

Milestone team members passing out Christmas presents at a local school

Year after year, Milestone team members will surprise customers or purchase the contents in people's shopping carts during the holidays. These are just a few ways Milestone stays true to their goal of making the most impact in the Dallas–Fort Worth community. Talk about a Win-Win-Win.

"When the team wins and the customer wins, the company wins," Gus says. This is evident through the many awards Milestone has won over the years. When Milestone was named number 4 of the Top 100 Places to Work in Dallas by the *Dallas Morning News* back in 2015, Gus and Mark were proud. Each year, the news visits the more than one thousand companies who submit an application and surveys their team. Milestone had made the list in previous years, but number 4 was the highest the company had ranked.

"We're doing something right," Mark told Gus. "The team has spoken." But Gus and Mark were not the only ones elated by the honor; everyone at Milestone felt proud to work there. They were buzzing about the number 4 spot for weeks!

Milestone has also won customer choice awards for ten years straight. These measures of talent retention and profitability earned Milestone awards from Southern Methodist University and *Inc.* magazine's "Inc. 5000" list for the company's growth.

Team member surveys and nationally recognized awards will always serve as evidence of Win-Win-Win in action. But the most important pieces of evidence are found in customer satisfaction and a little thing known as "the pickle."

Milestone tech sharing booties with a cute customer!

Robert Dull Brandon Preusser Shane Greenlee Eliana McGrath
Vicente Martinez Savannah Forrest Frank Mattaliano Aaron Lee
Rohan Buck John Mendoza Joey Barrientos Joshua Hessert Isaac
Norman Reid Runnels Edward Bell Hieu Thai Govani Aguilar
Michael Pottorff Justin Kelly Makayla Thomas Juan Esparza Ken-
neth Guthrie Carrie Petroski Gary Sparks Bobby Hobbs Nick Davis
Cooper Barksdale Austin Rogers Darius Williams Jaime Torres
Tashalynn Spraglin Parker Gregg Tevita Fetokai Patrick Malouf
Justin Tidwell Ryan McQuagge Ed Elkhenfas Glen Hallihan Cassidy
Bender Mike Fortner Josh
Weemes David Klutsey Eliu
Flores BrandonClark David
Shroyer Michael Caldwell   Becca Jimenez
Juan Mejia Erick Rodri- guez Steven Proctor Brandon
Eason Adam Arredondo Fredrick Burks Christopher Vega Ibra-
him Widyan Jimmie Huckeba Scott Henry Danny White Steven
Basques Michael Rosebrock Justin Witte Jacob Ehlen Margarito Padilla
Nicholas Clem Mario Centeno David Kinney James Wann Kristi Jones
Sheridian   Wyatt Nancy Brockelman Daryle For-
                                   rest Bryan Valenta Chase Schultz
                                   Johnny Clark William Walker
                                   David White Brandon Mayfield
                                   Tim Weisser Spencer Burchinal
                                   Jared Wright Sheldon Roy Chace
McLeod   Robert Latchaw Jodie Lemmon
Ernst Schar Dillon   Fryer Bryan Clark Desiree Jensen
Oscar Prieto Jenifer Hampton Reed Chenault Daniel Boles Caitlyn Williams
Colton Seeton Jennifer Porter Christopher Shriver Branton Harden Carlos
Jasso Lee Wonzo Aaron Mosqueda Jackson Vogels Heather Smith Bruce
Freeman Kimberly Macias John Katchinska Julia Selke Johnathan
McCoy Ken Marshall Jaimee Kirby Johnny Vasquez Kelly Kinkade
Charles Dozeman Morgan Jarvis Charles Schellhase Ryan
Lopez Steven Smith Jason Ethridge Kameron
Kirk Nicholas McDaniel

GIVE 'EM THE PICKLE!

Remember this: Whoever sows sparingly will also reap sparingly, and whoever sows generously will also reap generously. Each of you should give what you have decided in your heart to give, not reluctantly or under compulsion, for God loves a cheerful giver.

—2 Corinthians 9:6–8 NIV

**"Remember, our business is not what we sell. It is who we serve,"
Bob Farrell said after dancing around the television screen holding a pickle.** "You and I are in the people business."

Gus and Mark nodded.

They certainly were.

For those unfamiliar, Bob Farrell of Farrell's Ice Cream Parlour and Restaurant is a customer service icon. His training video "Give 'Em the Pickle"[4] has been shared as a training tool all over the country. It is also a book by the same name. After Gus and Mark saw that video of Bob, they purchased the training DVD to show their team members.

The lesson is simple. Farrell received a letter from a beloved customer who wrote about how they had been coming to Farrell's since it opened. They loved the food, especially the pickles (the customer claimed Farrell's had the best pickles in Seattle). On a recent visit, they requested extra pickles. It was a common request, usually granted without a fuss. This time, the waitress said, "I can bring you a side of pickles, but that will be seventy-five cents."

The customer never had to pay for extra pickles before. It was a bit of a disappointment. They wrote to Farrell, and that letter served as the ultimate motivation behind Farrell's "Give 'Em the Pickle" customer service training.

The training poses a simple question: *What is more important: earning three quarters for those pickles or giving the customer what they want and expect?* If pickles make them happy, give them the pickle!

The pickle became a service industry symbol of giving the customer a little something extra or unexpected to deliver a positive experience. Businesses have the right to ask their customers to pay for what they're getting, but if you "give them the pickle," it shows you're going the extra mile to make people happy.

Giving the pickle means not worrying about the little stuff, which is why Milestone encourages technicians to do something a little extra for every customer. Doing this benefits the technicians, too. Milestone has a weekly Pickle Award for whoever gave the best "pickle" to a customer. Most technicians work in two-man teams. Therefore, one team member

---

4 "Give 'Em the Pickle by Bob Farrell—Customer Service Training," Media Partners, posted May 4, 2011, YouTube video, 3:51, https://www.youtube.com/watch?v=ISJ1V8vBiil.

will take a photo or video documenting the unexpected act of service. The stories are great.

One time, a technician was on a call and the customer was very ill. Their Chihuahua, Chico, was moping by the front door, hoping to go for a walk. The technician asked the customer if he could walk Chico after he completed the job. On another call, an elderly lady wanted to put up a large Christmas tree but couldn't do it herself and didn't have anyone who could do it for her. Technicians Steven and Michael set up her Christmas tree, lights and all. That extra act of kindness meant a lot to her, and it was completely unexpected.

Caption from post by Aaron Behunin on Feb. 25: "Sharing this shout-out for Aaron and Bailey! Not only did they serve the customer with excellence, but they took down his Christmas lights! Talk about going above and beyond! Great job, guys! Keep up the great work! Thank you, Gus Antos."

Milestone had another elderly customer whose dog escaped from her home after the wind blew open the door to her garage. Her technician, Tyler, helped her retrieve the escapee and then repaired the door so her dog could not make a run for it again.

In the middle of summer, Marcus pulled up to a gas station and noticed two women trying to change a flat tire. Being the Milestone "pickle giver" that he is (his words), he happily changed their tire for them under the hot Texas sun.

In October 2018, Billy and Adam stopped to help a lady who was involved in a hit-and-run accident. She was not in immediate danger, so the guys knew not to move her from the vehicle. As she sat in her car trying to process what had happened, they stayed by her side, offering support until first responders arrived.

Sometimes the pickle can be serendipitous. A Milestone customer had a crack in his driveway that he was going to call someone to patch up. The technician had a little concrete in his truck left over from a previous job, so he patched the crack. The customer walked up to him and said, "Every Milestone employee that has come out to this house always goes above and beyond."

And sometimes, God places Milestone technicians exactly where they need to be. One November, a woman called for service at her home. When her technicians arrived, they could tell she seemed a little down. She avoided eye contact and seemed a little standoffish. Instead of chalking up her behavior to a bad day, her technicians took time to talk with her, not just about the service job but also about how life was going in general. By the end of the visit, she seemed a little better. They told her to have a great day and went on to the next service call.

Days later, Milestone received a compliment they would never forget. The woman from a few days prior took time to send in a note thanking Milestone for their service. "To be honest, I was considering taking my life the day Milestone arrived to my home. After talking with the guys, I felt differently," she wrote. Gus and Mark couldn't believe it.

"You can't make this stuff up," Eric said. The team applauded their technicians for a job well done and used that story to show how a little kindness can make a big impact on someone's life. It was the highest of compliments, and no one at Milestone would ever forget it.

Like Bob Farrell, Milestone feels the impact team members make when satisfied customers send in letters. Milestone keeps a booklet with all their customers' letters from over the years. The team knows they're doing something right when they receive ones that start out like this:

Dear Gus & Mark,

I want you to know that Carl is the best service person I ever had! He was on time with a smile on his face and his booties on. He was charming and professional and he knew what he was doing. He was able to make me understand what was going on. Now I think the fact that I had dumb & dumber with the cable folks here at the same time, tracking mud all over the place, those two couldn't find their hiney with both hands, did make Carl look like Albert Einstein. That being said, Carl was just wonderful and I won't let anyone but Carl work on my units. Bravo guys, you picked a peach.

Sometimes Milestone technicians reach out to Mark and Gus to determine if they can give an extraordinary pickle to a customer in need.

Dear Mark and Gus,

It's our great pleasure to let you know how pleased we are with Milestone. Most companies are out mainly to make money, rightly expected, of course. The statement does not reflect your establishment. It is obvious that you put your customers' needs first.

This customer went on to applaud the work of technicians Kevin and Chris, who spent three and a half hours in their home. The family was having a tough time financially and expected the bill to be around $350. During that three-and-a-half-hour service call, Kevin and Chris determined the family was facing a financial hardship (our technicians get to know our customers while on the job). Chris gave Gus and Mark a quick call—which they encourage the guys to do—and explained the situation. After talking it over, Gus told him to tear up the invoice.

If you go with your gut, you'll do the right thing, and if you do the right thing, your customers will tell the world. That is the case with the customer who wrote that letter. She told her family, friends, and anyone who would listen how Milestone was there for her and her husband in their time of need.

Sometimes Milestone's impact is so profound, the team learns that they've touched customers' lives in ways they could never imagine. One customer wrote a letter that really made the whole team appreciate the value of the pickles.

Her letter read as follows:

> My husband just passed away and I had no idea how I was going to deal with the situation in my home until you guys came out. The technician went above and beyond explaining stuff to me. As a widow, I know my husband is looking down happy that Milestone is in my life.

That one-on-one connection is priceless. Even though Milestone gets to serve individuals and families daily, they also provide the same level of service and "pickles" to local businesses.

One year, Milestone completed a huge job for a nonprofit youth development center, dedicated to helping kids who don't have anywhere to go for the short term. The center provided transitional housing and enrichment for at-risk youth. Gus and Mark went out to the site and discovered someone had stolen the electrical panel on the side of their building.

"What happened?" Gus asked the director of the program.

"We have no idea," she replied, "but we don't know how we're going to pay for a replacement. We need air conditioning for the residents as well. It's a mess."

"We'll send some techs out to get you guys up and running," Gus said.

The next morning, Gus sent out a technician who did around $4,000 worth of work. The day after the service was complete, the director came to Milestone's office with a check. Gus and Mark took it for processing, but they knew they weren't going to cash it. Instead, they wrote "VOID" all over the check and returned it to the director with a little note:

This is our way of helping out.

The director was shocked.

"You guys have no idea how much of an impact you made. We never expected this. Thank you," the director told them upon receiving the note.

These acts of kindness are part of who the team is. From the earliest days, the company's goal has been to directly impact people's lives for the better. To do that, they're going to treat people right. They're going to seize the moments to create memorable experiences.

Customers will forget the work you did, the price of the job, maybe even your name, but they will never forget the way you made them feel. Try to make everyone feel special. That's the Milestone way.

As business owners, you have plenty to worry about on a day-to-day basis. In business and in life, don't sweat the small stuff, and when you make sure you do right by your customers, the company wins, too.

Just give 'em the pickle. It's worth it.

Caption from post by Byron Byars on October 3, 2018: "Brought groceries in for an eighty-year-old couple. His wife ate the Crunch 'n Munch on the way home (not me!)."

Scott Huggett David Evans Bryan Dun-
gan Phil Richey Dawn Trevino Leigh
Ann Drane Roland Rios Taylor Sullivan
Jordan Dixon Aaron Andrews Darrel
Martin Carlie Mikeska Marcos Maldo-
nado Corey Griffin Abel Lomas Dustin
Merimon Ashley LaRoe Eric Wright
Christian Keith Ricardo Macias Lori
Stone Marco Lara Nathaniel Young
Manuel Escobar Tyler Wright Jason
Haygood Stephen Colbaugh Ryan Hall Geno Duran Jose
Puga Russell Coleman Blane Russell Hannah Weidman Ruben Pe-
rez Emily Tate Chris Runyon Gabriel Guerrero Gage Thompson Thomas
Birtch Isidro Torres Randy Baltazar Victor Carrillo Bobby Stiefer Joshua
Byrd Eric Castillo Luke Wilken James Howard Kelsey Synatschk Bobby LeFlore
Albert Rodriguez Abner Fuentus Kevin Worden Jason Bell Linda Keeton Victor
Reyes Melissa Pollard Marcus Walker   Joshua Malone Zachery Stinson
Chris Bruton Ronald Barrett John   McLanahan John Mongin Evan
Daniel Blaine Boyle James Spoon   Charles Looper Jessica Keels
Gustavo Cisneros Rudy Serna   Miguel Mier Teresa Wilder David
Wilson Terry Sasser Robert   Wallis Brett Tidwell Michael
Simmons Jezenia Silva Yosimar   Pineda Dustin Stratton Amy
Singh Edward Parvin Dom-   inique Richardson John Cordero
Casey Simpson Patrick Latona   Adam Zamora Rey Maldonado
Simon Torres Erin Vetter Max   Berber Kristopher Washington
Michael Palomino Joseph Lobin Juan Herrera Alan Beltran Nathan Reeves Adam
Tellez Colton Maples Johnny Gutierrez Nena Stewart Joseph Ward Tracy Wilson
Adam Stockton Jimmy Rayo Billy Joel Funderburg Cody Hopson Charles
Oneal George Herrell Nicholas Hughes Phillip Herrington Michael
Woolheater Alyssa Sullivan Robert Aguilar Ronald Daniels Kyle
Calame Jonathan Ray Humberto Pincheira Kyle Parker
Kulin Honeycutt Lukas Landry Kenneth McGa-
hee Dawn Wright Byron Hepler Matilde
Gomez Nicholas Barnes

INVESTING IN PEOPLE—RISK AND REWARD

**Either make the tree good and its fruit good,
or make the tree bad and its fruit bad;
for the tree is known by its fruit.**

—Matthew 12:33 NIV

The pickles help Milestone team members see the value of their work and service. Team members take pride in what they do. In turn, Milestone invests a lot of time and resources in finding the right people. But not every story of someone joining Milestone—or any company—is pie-in-the-sky perfect.

A long time ago, Gus and Mark hired a technician, Greg, who consistently did a good job. They needed someone to help manage the technicians, so they promoted him. Greg was the first person within Milestone promoted up through the trade from technician to a leadership position, a great example of what happens when a job is done through hard work and excellence. That is, until Greg started to falter on the excellence part.

Gus and Mark got word that Greg's marriage was in trouble. He'd walk into the office, shoulders slightly slumped, barely speaking to his colleagues, and everyone could tell something was wrong. Greg began spending time with the Milestone team chaplain, which was good, but it wasn't enough.

A few months went by, and Gus and Mark learned that Greg—who was still married—liked another woman at the office. That rumor turned out to be true. Greg and a female colleague engaged in an affair within their faith-based company. The new couple must have known Gus and Mark would not approve. It went against Milestone's values and created a lot of negative experiences, including gossip and secrecy. Of course, Gus and Mark didn't find out until later, so they were not in a position to address it at the time.

Around the same time, Milestone was experiencing significant growth. When Greg knocked on Gus's open door on a Friday afternoon, Gus didn't expect what came next.

"Excuse me, Gus. I need a word," Greg said as he appeared in the doorway of the office. He looked nervous.

"Go on," Gus said.

Greg was beet red, a bead of sweat dripping from his brow. "I'm, I'm going to have to quit. I, uh, want to do something else with my life."

Gus shifted in his seat and took his eyes off the computer screen, giving Greg his full attention. "Hm," Gus paused and took a full breath. "Where's this coming from? I thought you were happy here."

"I don't know. It, uh, it is just what I need to do right now."

"Okay, you know what's best for you," Gus said. Greg shuffled out of the office.

It all seemed so odd. Gus was puzzled, for sure.

When Monday came, Greg did not report to work, and then Gus and Mark found out his girlfriend did not show up for her shift either. They assumed the pair quit so they could continue their affair. It was far worse than that. A guy recruited Greg to start a new service company in the area. It was nearly identical to Milestone but had a different name. Greg started trying to recruit Milestone technicians, while his girlfriend tried to recruit call-takers.

Over the course of Milestone's history, it has been very rare that someone has left to work for a peer or competitor simply because they did not want to work at Milestone. When people leave Milestone, it is usually for a life change, such as moving to a new area, going back to school full time, or changing industries. Seventy percent of the time, it's Milestone who ends the relationship. When things don't work out, the Culture and Care team work with the individual, plugging them into different roles until they found out what works. If nothing works, that person is promoted to customer.

Gus and Mark were livid in the wake of the betrayal. To have someone they invested so much time and money in just turn around and stab them and all of Milestone in the back was infuriating. Unfortunately, things got worse.

During his tenure at Milestone, Greg had stolen documents, folders, invoices, pricing systems, and pricing books. These things took years to develop and perfect, and Gus and Mark learned that before Greg left, he took the Milestone logo off the materials and put a new logo on for his "new" company. He sent documents and files to advertising companies to create his overtly copied marketing collateral. Worst of all, he had been planning this betrayal for quite some time.

Gus and Mark filed a cease and desist order. They told him, "If you want to go do your own thing, go for it, but don't do *our* thing that we paid you to learn. Don't try to steal our team members."

Ultimately, they won the lawsuit, and Greg's copycat company lasted six months before it went under. Gus, Mark, and the whole Milestone team were devastated by the experience.

You don't have to be Billy Graham to work at Milestone, but the second you start to pull in a direction opposite of the company's mission and values, it is time to go.

Building People, Not Business

Starting and growing a company will always come with risks. Sometimes you will make the right decision, and sometimes you will not. When you don't, you chalk up the experience as a teachable moment and remember the lesson as you move forward. There will always be wrong-fitting people who slip by you. The best thing you can do is listen when people tell you there is a problem, put out the fire as quick as you can, and never let someone who wrongs you change your vision.

Milestone is a tree, and its people are the fruit. Gus and Mark want to nourish and grow the best fruit so everything team members do is done with excellence and a kind heart. Ninety percent of Milestone's training is on communication. One of the most effective ways they've discovered to teach this is through Milestone's Top Gun School.

It was 1:55 p.m. as Dennis pulled the Milestone van up to a large white house. He double-checked his GPS to make sure he was at the correct residence and took a deep breath as he mentally ran through a list of things he would need to do. He checked his hair in the rearview mirror, shut the van off, and walked up to the front door.

Dennis looked for a doorbell but did not see one, so he knocked three times in quick succession. After the final knock, he took a step backward to give the customer space when she opened the door.

Smile. Keep your hands out of your pockets. Explain what you are here to do, Dennis told himself.

The door flew open.

"Hello, Mrs. Chambers. My name is Dennis from Milestone, and I will be inspecting that ceiling fan light that has been giving you trouble," Dennis said.

"I've been expecting you. Come on in," Mrs. Chambers replied.

Dennis stepped across the threshold and onto the indoor welcome mat. He grabbed his shoe protectors from his bag and slipped them over his shiny black boots so to not track dirt into the customer's home.

"I'll show you which one," Mrs. Chambers said as she led Dennis up the front stairs to the second floor.

For the next twenty minutes, Dennis meticulously examined the fixture, diagnosed the issue, rewired the fan, and double-checked the remaining fans in the home, even though he was only responsible for one. As the service visit came to a close, Dennis thanked Mrs. Chambers for choosing Milestone and turned to exit the home.

"Okay, I think that is the end," Mrs. Chambers said as Dennis reached out to open the door. He turned and smiled.

"How do you think I did?"

The woman smiled. "A-plus. The guys are upstairs with the recording. Down the hall and in that back room we didn't go into."

Mrs. Chambers was really an actress named Kathy, who was hired to play a customer for Milestone's Top Gun School. The school is a staged home where newly hired technicians perform a mock service visit from beginning to end. The entire process is recorded by cameras throughout the house. At the end of the test, the new team member goes to a room and watches a replay of the visit. This gives him or her the opportunity to see their performance as well as receive feedback on areas for improvement before interacting with a real customer.

Milestone used to conduct classroom trainings but found new team members were easily confused by the hypotheticals. All the classroom training in the world won't adequately prepare a technician for the real thing. The house has proven to be a great training tool and investment for the Milestone family. Also, it is a lot of fun.

Long-time Milestone team member Scott J., heading out for his first service call of the day

Training is not the only way to honor team members' commitment to the company, especially since compensation is always a factor in whether people stay or leave. In general, Milestone strives to pay 15–20 percent more than the competition. Gus and Mark can preach the message of the mission and values each and every day, but action speaks the loudest. They get really excited when they have the opportunity to reward people for hard work. In addition to pay, Gus and Mark give awards at company breakfasts, offer bonuses where applicable, and have been fortunate to witness team members grow within Milestone to leadership positions.

If they're not at Milestone, they'll be somewhere else. The only thing worse than training somebody and having them leave is not training them and having them stay. From a faith perspective, Milestone is called to train individuals and offer them the opportunity to learn and grow and to live their best lives. It all goes back to the Golden Rule: Treat others as you want to be treated.

Gus and Mark recognize the risk inherent in this. They know they could be developing resources within a person for competitors to steal. But if someone does leave, Gus and Mark want the receiving company to think, "Wow, Milestone did a great job with this one." Milestone can be a launching pad to bigger things, and Gus and Mark realize that. But if the goal is to always be the best place to work, Gus and Mark will focus on why someone would want to leave and how they can solve that problem.

Hiring new people is expensive, and training them is time-consuming, but Gus and Mark have learned that when you invest everything you can into people, it is absolutely worth it. If Milestone can touch someone in a positive and life-affirming way, then it is a success whether that individual stays or goes.

One example is Josh Moran, a long-time family friend of Gus. They went to the same school and the same church growing up. Not long after his twenty-seventh birthday, Josh decided he wanted to move out to California and plant a church in Calabasas. While he was out there, he took a job with a film editing company to bring in some money. He worked hard and learned a lot, gradually moving up in the company. During this time, Josh's wife gave birth to their son prematurely. Things got stressful without the support of immediate family, so Josh and his wife decided to move back to Dallas.

Josh called Gus one afternoon in 2005.

"Is anyone hiring?"

"I'll keep an eye out. We're trying to promote this electrical service company called Milestone," Gus offered. "I could use a graphic designer and someone who knows marketing. Are you interested?"

Josh was brought on as a contracted creative and became instrumental in Milestone's marketing efforts during a massive growth period. He worked on Milestone's advertisements, logos, and even its website. He was a godsend.

Like most people do after staying in one place for a time, Josh started wondering what his future could be. He wasn't an employee of Milestone, and it didn't look like he'd be joining full time. Josh sat down and told Gus he was ready to start his own company. Gus was thrilled. Milestone would be losing Josh, but the industry would gain an exceptional creative mind. Gus felt Milestone was serving as a launch pad for Josh in the best way. Today Josh's company does marketing for nearly three hundred other companies like Milestone across the United States. Josh is also a pastor of a small church, so he's living out two passions.

Before Josh went on to start his own company, he brought in Travis for an interview. When he started, Travis was eighteen years old and recently married, and he worked at a church doing graphic design. Gus and Mark hired him for about $30,000 a year. He stayed and grew with Milestone over the years. Today Travis is the type of guy where if something happens at Milestone, he feels like it is happening to him. He bleeds red and yellow and keeps Milestone in his heart at all times.

"My goal for you is not that you work here for the rest of your life. But when you do leave, you leave a better person," Gus told Travis. But Travis didn't leave. Today, he is Milestone's marketing manager, supervises a team of ten people, and spearheads all marketing efforts with passion and purpose. Gus and Mark firmly believe God must have sent Josh and Travis their way.

Some may scoff at investing as much training, development, time, and dollars into team members as Milestone does. But it works. People don't join Milestone to grow and leave like they do with many other companies. They grow to stay.

Josh and Travis were logical hiring choices based on their character. They *knew* someone at Milestone who could vouch for them. In 2008,

Gus and Mark made an unprecedented decision. It was time to look outside their network for a new hire. This individual would take on a huge leadership position within Milestone. They had to pick the right person.

Gus and Mark thought it over. They prayed. They consulted their church and community network but could not find a fit. Many employees were drawn to Milestone or were handpicked by Gus and Mark. Then they read Joe's resume. Joe had a big corporate background as a regional manager for a Stanley Steamer franchise. Wanting a change, he decided to apply for a general manager position with Milestone. Gus and Mark had lunch with Joe, and he impressed them with his expertise and business etiquette. Joe would be coming from a huge business. At this time, Milestone had about fifteen trucks on the road and was still trying to grow.

After that informal lunch and a formal Milestone interview, Joe was offered the position. Gus and Mark could tell he aligned with the Milestone mission. They trusted God and their guts, and it paid off in a big way. Joe turned out to be instrumental in Milestone's growth and success as Milestone's general manager, a role he still holds today.

Joe relied on his big corporate background to fine-tune systems and processes and bring in additional revenue that Milestone needed. He knew how to run a big business, and Milestone was slowly turning into just that. Joe was instrumental in Milestone's growth and success.

It all boils down to helping people be as good as they can because choosing to stay with you shows they're willing to forego other opportunities. If they stay, you're doing something right. If they leave, you know you helped them and did right by them. Milestone has always been and will continue to be a place where team members grow in confidence, skills, and ability both personally and professionally. It serves as a launching pad for internal and external opportunities. If a team member moves on to a new venture, Milestone ensures that individual doesn't just leave. They leave better.

Growth and development with the Milestone team

Annual Awards breakfast

Victor Borbolla Shawn Olivarez Dylan Lavalley Danielle McConnico Adam Hill Ryan Faulk
Ted Brooks Kyvawn Williams Darcelle Smiley Jose Aguilera Maegan Plummer Chaz
Lothschutz Clayton Foley Jeffrey Pennington Zakkary Chapman Damien Pruitt Jacee
Taylor Kaleb Douglass Alastair Franklin Bijar Saleem Ashleigh Lara Shelby Bright
Justin Smith Francisco Albarran Tristan Reed Fuller Angela Mikayla Duncan David
Ramshur Jordan Nix Dallas Weidman Amanda Manning Jesse Crane William
LaRoe Jennifer Simpson Avery Fain Jose Espinoza Jeffery Rutherford William
Sostre Wesley Tweton Megan Crow Anson Wallace Jerad Markham Christian
Johnson Derek Otey Wyatt Hogan Paul Hobbs Steele Rouble Raul Salas
Brian Reger LaShonda James Shanna Nevil Juan Perez Brian Lachaney
Iman Castelow Michael Hardin
Aaron Muncy Aaron Loutner Mat-
thew Evans James Martin Jim
Birney Jose Mondragon Jonathan
Gaona Alexis Vargas Tiffany Ste-
vens Octavious Mcpherson Krystal
Rios Joseph Yarnall Joel Mackey
Christian Hernandez Mason Keels
Luis Acuna Justin Mummey Ryan
Benoit Brandon Howk Gary Holley
Brenna Dustin Justin Adams Frank
Sudovsky Jonathan Hammer Brian-
na Evick Michael McCall Deen Hop-
son Justin O'Quain Justin Smith
Edgar Chavez Savannah Debose
Greg Smith Troy Sheafer Drew
Holt Jonathan Cavagnaro Trevor
Satterwhite Scott Clark David Wil-
son Chris Trowbridge Delicia Arm-
stead Jordan Evans Matthew Sher-
man Amado Balderas Dawaune
Sykes Madeleine Widmer Armando
Cruz Ruben Torres Jesse Miller

MEASURING
FOR SUCCESS

But whoever looks intently into the perfect law that gives freedom, and continues in it—not forgetting what they have heard, but doing it—they will be blessed in what they do.

—James 1:25 NIV

While pickles represent a small, simple act of kindness delivered to the customer, it is customer feedback that has inspired some big company decisions. Throughout 2014 and 2015, Milestone continually received customer requests for plumbing services. Customers craved a "one-stop shop" for electrical, HVAC, and plumbing. Gus and Mark have always been receptive to customer and team feedback. In 2015, they decided to explore options for a plumbing service line. They had the perfect person in mind. His name was David.

David had known Gus and Mark for more than ten years. "If I ever decide to sell my company, I would want to sell to someone like Milestone. You've always been hospitable to other companies, whether they were competitors or not," David said to Gus one afternoon.

That conversation about possibility evolved into negotiations. Gus and Mark had a lot of confidence in Butler Plumbing. That company was a member of Success Group International (SGI), just like Milestone. In 2015, Butler Plumbing became Milestone Plumbing. Milestone accomplished the trifecta of residential services. David is still an integral part of Milestone and the plumbing sector of the company has grown year after year. Thanks to customer feedback, Milestone now does plumbing, HVAC, home security, window cleaning, and even garage door installation.

By listening to their customers, Gus and Mark learned that the most important thing to them is not services or price—it's *time*. They want to know when Milestone will show up and that technicians have everything they need to get the job done quickly and correctly. Most of the time, technicians can complete a job in one visit. This way, customers rarely worry about scheduling subsequent visits. Gus and Mark had to purchase larger vehicles capable of holding everything a technician might need for the job. The larger vehicles don't get the best gas mileage and cost more to operate, but having everything on the truck is better for the customer. What is best for the customer is best for Milestone.

After providing additional services and being on time, Gus and Mark learned communication is also very important to their customers. Customers didn't want to sit around and wonder whether they're going to get a call or email or unannounced knock on the door. The Milestone team surveyed customers to determine how they prefer to be contacted prior to service. Most request a simple text message. Some trade companies don't have that capability; Milestone certainly didn't when it started. Since customers made it clear how important this aspect was to them, Gus and Mark explored a variety of information technology and telecommunications vendors to determine if Milestone could develop a synchronized system.

If a technician is heading to a customer's home, the customer will receive a text that reads, "Tim from Milestone is on the way. He will be there in about forty-five minutes." The customer receives a link in the text they can use to respond. They can text back and say, "I'm running ten minutes late," and someone from Milestone will reply. It is a great system for technicians and customers (and also protects technicians from distracted driving).

Communication is equally important for team members. Many companies survey their customers to determine satisfaction of services, but Milestone also surveys team members. Gus, Mark, and the Culture and Care team want to know how satisfied their fellow team members are with their jobs, what Milestone as a company can do better, and if there is anything other organizations do that they'd like to see Milestone adopt. As mentioned before, people don't quit jobs; people quit bosses. Gus and Mark strive each day to make Milestone a place where people love coming to work. For that to happen, feedback is paramount. It didn't happen overnight, but Gus and Mark's transparency eventually built a foundation of trust across the Milestone family.

One summer day in 2016, Gus was walking between buildings on the Milestone campus. As the sweat dripped from his brow, he spotted a team member driving one of the Milestone trucks and flagged him down.

"Man, it's like 107 degrees right now. Can I hitch a ride?"

Gus hopped into the truck and asked his team member how he was doing. Not the generic "How are you?" but a real "How are you doing today?"

"I'm all right. How 'bout you?" the driver asked.

"I'm good now that I got this ride."

The two rode in silence before the technician pulled over and put the truck in park. He paused for a thoughtful moment. "Actually, I have a situation."

"What's up?" Gus angled his body toward him.

"I've got a great group of guys working with me, but I have one who just isn't pulling his weight. He calls out a lot, and my guys have to scramble to cover for him. I don't know if he has something going on or if he's trying to pull a fast one."

The revelation came from a place of trust. Gus easily could have tracked the technician in question. He could set up a meeting and try to get to the bottom of this man's callouts. Instead, Gus suggested something else.

"How about you and one of your guys take him out for lunch and see if he'll open up? You don't want to come from a place of blame, but you also need to let him know how his actions impact the team."

"That's a fine idea," the technician said as he drove Gus the rest of the way to the office building. That candid moment was a testament to Gus and Mark's leadership. They, along with Milestone's leadership team, had successfully created an environment where feedback is not only appreciated but also sought after.

Back in 2016, the Culture and Care team saw a trend where team members stated they were working too many hours. They wanted to spend more time at home with their families. Milestone used to be a six-day-a-week company, with Sundays off (except for emergencies). Today the company only operates Monday to Friday, with Saturday volunteer opportunities, because an overwhelming majority of our team members said, "If I could have Saturdays and Sundays to spend with my family, I would feel more compelled to stay at Milestone. Also, I'd do a better job Monday through Friday." Up until this point, technicians could take a weekday off if they worked a weekend, but the rest of the Milestone team didn't always have that option. If a department was short-staffed, managers would have to work weekends and throughout the week.

Making that change was a huge undertaking. Milestone had been open six days a week for years. But when so many team members gave the same feedback, Gus and Mark knew they had to listen. Situations and policies like these are constantly changing, but the important lesson is to constantly ask how our team is doing and be willing to make changes.

Getting honest feedback has been a "test and see" operation. In Milestone's early days, Gus used to pull ten to twenty newish team members into a meeting and ask them questions like "How do you like it here?" "Do you like your team leader?" "What is something that you would do better?" He got very few answers. Most team members responded with "Everything is great."

Except it wasn't. Someone from that survey group would quit a few days later. Gus would catch them in the hall and ask them, "You just told me everything was great. Why quit?" That's when he realized most people don't feel comfortable giving feedback in a face-to-face environment. He set the stage for failure because he didn't create a safe environment for people to be honest.

Once he figured that out, Gus discussed the process with Mark. The pair decided to send email surveys. That failed too. People ignored the email, and he wouldn't receive nearly enough responses to uncover issues and form action plans to address them. After two failed methods, Gus and Mark tried something new. They gathered team members together, put them in a room, placed a paper survey in front of them, and gave them twenty minutes to complete it. Gus and Mark encouraged anonymity—though it is not required—and asked them to place the completed survey in a box by the door when they finished. One hundred percent completion rate every time.

The Culture and Care team spearheads the satisfaction surveys today. Through trial and error, they learned to keep the surveys short. Each survey has five or six questions. They learned to ask the right questions too, such as "What is one thing you would change about Milestone?" and "What is one thing you've experienced at a previous employer that you would like to see at Milestone?" They take the results and input them into SurveyMonkey, which analyzes the responses. It works.

The process was not without additional lessons. Gus and Mark learned the hard way that you cannot confront someone about their negative feedback. Confrontation leads to a loss of trust. On one occasion, someone wrote, "I don't enjoy working with my manager, and I feel like Milestone has lost its values of Faith, Family, and Excellence." That stung. Because of the way the surveys were set up—*optionally anonymous*—Gus used the process of elimination and determined who the respondent was. Like any leader, he wanted to fix it, so he went to the individual, addressed the survey, and the employee went off and told everyone in the company if you write something bad, Gus will come talk to you about it. He never made that mistake again.

Surveys offer insightful lessons on self-awareness. For the team member, their perception is reality. Their feedback gives Milestone's leadership and Culture and Care team an opportunity to influence how respondents perceive situations at work.

To measure for success, consistency is key. Surveys are issued on the same day of the week, at the same time of the year. The team found that if a survey was distributed on a Friday versus a Monday, people responded in very different ways, depending on the day. On Friday, everything is wonderful, and people don't have a care in the world. On Monday, people are preparing for the work week and can pinpoint elements of their job they wish were different. Milestone avoids giving surveys out in the middle of summer because that is their busiest time. Calling people into a room when they've got calls and paperwork and a ton of other messages piling up in their inboxes results in rushed surveys and incomplete feedback. Just like Mondays versus Fridays, people needed to be in the right mindset to take their time and give honest answers to the questions.

Timing is everything. The Culture and Care team once compared survey results from March with results from July. In March, everyone said they loved working at Milestone. In July, everyone hated their work and wanted to quit. Eric and his team thought the place went to hell in a handbasket in just three months! Then he looked at the trends. Summer is insanely busy and stressful, whereas March is just normal busy. Now he knows to compare similar survey timeframes to get more accurate results.

Another lesson: comparison is key. The Culture and Care team used to ask team members how they would rate their benefits. Nearly everyone would say "not good." They changed the question to "How would you rate your benefits compared to places you've worked prior to this job?" The responses changed, significantly, with positive feedback. It wasn't Milestone's specific insurance that people were disappointed in but the insurance system as a whole. Maybe there was room for improvement, but team members were satisfied with their benefits compared to other places.

At the very end of the survey, respondents are asked, "How long do you see yourself continuing to be a team member at Milestone?" The options are "less than a year," "more than a year," and "5+ years." The overwhelming answer we get is "5+ years." They may have concerns, and the surveys help Milestone address those, but at the end of the day, respondents are happy with their jobs and want to stay.

Even after collecting this data regularly, Milestone takes it one step further by surveying team members' spouses. Gus and Mark want to make sure team members' spouses are satisfied with their partners' employment. Spouses are asked about their impression of Milestone. Spouse responses tend to be a bit unfiltered compared to those submitted by team members. That is because team members go home and vent. Spouse feedback gives a different and much-needed perspective.

Milestone starts building that relationship the day a new team member joins the family. The Culture and Care team gathers important information, such as the new member's birthday and anniversary and their spouse's and children's birthdays. On those dates, a card signed by the whole team and a gift card is mailed to the team member's house. It is not just a team member joining Milestone; their family joins too.

Techs in Milestone U-HVAC Academy

By now it should be clear how important that first team member Win of Win-Win-Win truly is. To foster team member happiness and fulfillment, Milestone recently started a mentorship program where new team members are assigned to a more seasoned team member for six months. During that time, the two team members have lunch together once or twice a month. Gus and Mark were inspired by their church and the way the church community welcomed new members and their families. They wanted to emulate that warm welcome and mentorship at Milestone.

This way, the new team member has a friend on day one. They can ask any questions they want without feeling stupid. For example, someone new might ask their mentor about Milestone's dress code policy. They might want to know if they can wear a brown belt instead of a black one. Those are the kinds of questions people feel awkward asking their supervisor. The mentorship program takes that pressure away and lets new team members feel comfortable at a peer level. It is all about helping people find connections in their work.

Within the first thirty days of hiring, the new team member will attend Culture Week with team members hired around the same time. During Culture Week, the team members will learn all the mission, values, and programs offered to the Milestone family. Culture Week encourages team member buy-in. It energizes team members to fully dive in and get excited about who Milestone is, where the company came from, and where Milestone is headed.

Throughout the week, the new team members will connect with one another through icebreakers. Sometimes they will participate in a scavenger hunt throughout the office. Instead of finding items, participants seek out team members with specific interests. A clue could be "This electrician plays in a rock band on the weekends," and the participants will talk to all the electricians to find the one mentioned in the clue. It is fun to watch.

At ninety days, it is essential to make sure the new hire is the right person for the company and that Milestone is the right company for them. About 30 percent of people hired are gone in the first ninety days. The Culture and Care team conducts a review (the new team member will be more open with someone other than their direct team leader), asking questions such as "Do you enjoy working here?" "Does the job meet your expectations?" "Do you know what our values are?" "Do you see yourself working here in a year?" "What brings you joy outside of Milestone?" They use this time to check on the team member as a person, not just an employee.

Gus and Mark wanted team members to feel they had someone to talk to beyond their supervisor. They understood that talking about personal things could seem intimidating, so they brought on Scott, the first Milestone chaplain, to provide general counseling and support for team members. Scott was friends with Gus's parents when he was a kid. Scott also knew Mark and Sabrina because they all went to the same church back in the late '80s.

Gus and Mark appreciated the oddity of having a company chaplain at a residential services company. But they knew it was important. Scott's only job was to be there for team members and make sure they were physically, spiritually, and mentally healthy. If a team member wanted to pay off his house, Scott would sit down with him and help him find a financial planner. If someone wanted to take their family to Disney World, Scott would help them find a travel agent.

Scott stayed on the team for several years before leaving to create his own consulting business. Gus and Mark gave him their blessing and wished him success, since Scott was a huge asset to Milestone. Wanting to fill Scott's shoes, Gus and Mark set off to hire a new chaplain. They ended up partnering with former Cowboys and Patriots player Eugene Lockhart, who today is the Milestone chaplain.

From customer feedback to service line requests to team member surveys and personal check-ins, measuring satisfaction and fulfillment will always be a priority at Milestone. Each dataset leads to new discoveries and improvement. That is why it is paramount to ask questions and listen to the answers provided. A know-it-all attitude leaves no room for growth. And incredible things manifest from growth.

A small part of the Milestone team that make success happen day after day!

Christian Smith
Lauren Hardin Brandon Bowden
Bryan Rourke Josh Edwards Shawn Wright
Jonathan Widmer Trevor Jeffers Sarah Thomas Paige
Hubacek Lauren Jacobsen Mandy Maknojia Andrew LeTour-
neau Henry Gotcher Camren Crouch Shan Bullard Jason Hobson Les
Adair Matthew Glenn Emilee DuBois Richard Mesler Reggie Jones Willie
Stroman Christian Sweet Miguel Rodriguez Dany Cendejas Michael Laur

Jonathan Stout Clint Winston Mar- cos Medina Christopher LeFevre
Shane McDaniel Fernando Torres Juan Perez David Butler Clar-
ence Andrews Jerry Eades Tara Barnes Ricardo Landa Sheylon
Stine John Guerrero William Hopkins Hugo Sanchez Juan
Puente Quincy Kent Bill Bryan Andrew Mullins Joey Cobble
Dacius Smith Antelmo Lubiano Andrew Mizell Andre Sanchez

Alicia Farrar Caitlin Compton Nick Kea Seth Lynch Kristen McDavid
Brandon Williams Jonathan Bailey Ryne Bergren Brenton White
Cole Newsom Willliam Rudnisky Shaun Brown
Bailey Archer Ricardo Martinez Humberto Puga
Johnny Alvarado Alesha Cook Stefan Ybarra Omar Salinas
Tallen Contreras Cody Moss William Tate Anthony Carmona Jose An-

tunez Scott Pomelow Michael Bagley Aaron Serna Sanjin
Vrbnjak Marshall Manning Tori Chatagnier Alan Arias Joshua
Baker Henry Diaz Jimmy Pierce Jose Arizpe Morgan Johnston
Lisa Anderson Floyd Crook Javier Eguia Aaron Hernandez Clinton
Nevil Federico Nunez Harry Ward Cody Martin Kevin Nickel
Margaux Holland Rigoberto Perez William Busby Jasmine Vasquez
Ashley Jones Timothy Chalfant Ty- ler Weidman Hakar Mustafa Keith

Reynolds Landon Williams Zachary Kennedy Jorge Mejorado Carl Thomas
Wesley Floyd Brandon Hines Robert Short Tyler Holleman Andy Lopez Ali
Simpson Hailey Norwood Luke Penny Jackie Arbaiza Maegan Skinner Aaron
Moriarity Andrew Loyd Reyes Mercado Bailey Isom Joel Gonzalez Zach-
ary Zajdl Montel Lee Craig Brown David Davila David O'Connor
Antonio Gayton Michael Rivera Ronaldis Calderon
Yolanda Trujillo Jorge Ruiz Gilbert Edwards
Chris Grammer

CULTIVATE YOUR RELATIONSHIPS

Do nothing out of selfish ambition or vain conceit. Rather, in humility value others above yourselves, not looking to your own interests but each of you to the interest of others.

—Philippians 2:3–4 NIV

Throughout Milestone's growth, Gus and Mark know God has placed certain people in their path for a reason. While Milestone works hard to attract humble, hungry, and smart people to the team, the company's service approach and dedication to the community inspires unique networking opportunities along the way. Sometimes, these networking opportunities are so serendipitous, they changed the course of Milestone's journey. That is exactly what happened when Mark and Gus met Jimmie.

It was 2007, and Milestone won their first Dallas Consumers' Choice Award. At that time, there were eight service trucks in the fleet. During the awards banquet, a tall man with dark hair and a big smile approached the table.

"Hi, I'm Jimmie. What do you guys do?" he asked.

"We're Milestone Electric," Gus replied.

"Nice. I have a plumbing company called Baker Brothers."

"You have got to be kidding me. Ha!" Gus said with a grin.

Gus and Mark were very familiar with Baker Brothers. At the time, they had twelve to fifteen trucks in their fleet. Gus and Mark looked up to that company in a way. Baker Brothers was well established and well respected in the community.

"I would love to get together sometime and pick your brain," Gus told him.

"Absolutely. Just let me know."

"Jimmie, where do you live?"

"I live in Rockwall."

"No kidding. Mark and I live in Rockwall."

For context, Rockwall is the smallest county in Texas. Talk about a small world. Turns out, the guys all lived a mile from each other.

That simple greeting was the beginning of a mutually beneficial relationship. This was before Gus and Mark added plumbing to Milestone's services. Therefore, Milestone and Baker Brothers were hardly competitors. In fact, Jimmie was always willing to share information about the industry. Gus and Jimmie became great friends, as did their wives.

Then one day, Gus received a call from a marketing agency. They were sending a representative to the Dallas–Fort Worth area who specialized in home services. Gus wanted Jimmie to connect with the representative. He saw a marketing opportunity Milestone should take advantage of.

Milestone Mark at the State Fair of Texas showing the signature "arm swoosh"

This trick-or-treater was spotted on Halloween dressed as Milestone Mark!

Baker Brothers was leaps ahead of Milestone in terms of marketing and advertising. They traveled to the local ABC TV network headquarters to meet the representative, Craig. Craig seemed to think it was a bit unusual to talk with two different companies at the same time, but Gus and Jimmie told him two heads were better than one. He couldn't argue with that.

Craig laid out a plan that basically said if Milestone went on television, the business would explode, and he had the numbers to back it up. For $30,000 a month, Gus and Mark would be able to run some well-placed ads and get a high return on investment.

Though Milestone was bringing in more business than during their Rainbow Truck days, thirty grand was still a lot of money. If Gus and Mark signed on for two months and it didn't work, it could be financially catastrophic. They wouldn't necessarily go out of business, but that massive size of an investment carried a lot of risk.

Jimmie and Gus weighed the pros and cons over several breakfasts and lunches. Mark and Gus went back and forth about the business plan Craig developed. They had seen several other companies doing television advertisements in other markets, and at the time, Milestone's revenue was about $5 million annually.

"We'd be doubling our marketing overnight," Mark said.

Even though they were nervous about taking the leap, they decided to go for it.

Milestone ran advertisements for one month and got a little exposure. It didn't blow the business out of the marketing waters, but more people were shown Milestone's message than if they hadn't run the ads. For the second month, Gus returned to the station and tweaked some of the ads and scheduling. They saw the same results and signed on for a third month. Then it took off. Milestone was *flooded* with calls.

Gus and Mark were ready to sign on for a fourth month of advertising when the unthinkable happened: the economic crash of 2008. The stock market plummeted, and the Great Recession began.

They were at a crossroads. The advertising was working, and they were seeing results, but was it worth investing during troubling economic times? They considered scaling back because they weren't sure how effective advertising would be. On the one hand, there would be businesses out there that wouldn't spend as much money as they would if the economy was fine. On the other hand, if they advertised to the people spending money, they could gain the upper hand on competitors who pulled out of advertising due to the recession.

After a few meetings, Gus and Mark added a new television station. National brands were scaling back advertising, which made stations desperate to sell their empty airtime slots. Advertising package prices dropped by nearly half the going rate. It was the perfect time to make this investment. Milestone would be one of the few local voices still on television at a bargain.

Looking back, God was opening doors before Gus and Mark even knew what was happening.

On the first day of filming their new commercial, a long-time Milestone electrician, Mark C., came by the set.

"Hey Mark, why don't you jump in and lip-sync the jingle we made?" Gus asked him. "You could do a little swoosh of your arm as you do it."

Mark C. laughed. Without hesitation, he jumped in.

"Milestone Electric. We fix it in a flash," Mark said with gusto.

Funnily enough, Mark's spontaneous appearance made the final cut. Gus didn't know it then, but Mark C. and the jingle would eventually become one of the most recognizable elements of Milestone. If a technician wears his uniform or logo anywhere in Dallas–Fort Worth, people will come up and sing the jingle. And Mark? Well, he unintentionally became Milestone's spokesperson: Milestone Mark.

Gus decided to have a little fun with the ads, so during Thanksgiving, Milestone Mark held pumpkins. If it was near Christmas, he'd wear a Santa hat. If they ran ads during football season, Mark would hold a football. He became a local celebrity. To this day, people regularly ask him for his autograph. If he goes out to lunch or dinner, people offer to pay for his meal. It is amazing. Milestone is lucky to have such a great guy on the team for so long.

But media is only one element of Milestone's marketing strategy. Gus and Mark wanted the commercials to show that Milestone was a small, hometown company. To do this, they ran ads at a very high frequency in a very short amount of time. On Monday and Tuesday, two weeks out of the month on any one station, viewers would see an abundance of Milestone commercials. It worked. They started getting calls and leads left and right.

Milestone expanded to other television stations and ended up broadcasting on all four major networks. In a two-year period, the company became one of the most recognized brands in the Dallas–Fort Worth area. Now if you wear a Milestone logo as far away as Atlanta, Georgia, people will come right up to you and sing the jingle!

Looking back, Gus and Mark had no idea that simple conversation with Jimmie at an awards banquet would lead Milestone to become the marketing powerhouse it is today. It is safe to say Milestone earned Jimmie's respect just as other business owners have throughout the years.

The advice tables turned when a local garage door company owner came to Milestone for some marketing advice. Always wanting to pay it forward, Gus and Mark happily obliged. After their meeting, the woman was so impressed with the way Milestone welcomed her and offered workable ideas, she offered the guys a garage door tune-up as a thank you for their time.

Three years later, Gus received a random voicemail from that same woman. She was done with her business, Welborn Garage Doors. "If there is one company I would want to buy me out, it's Milestone," she said on the message. Gus invited her back to the office for a meeting, and Milestone acquired her business. Granted, Gus and Mark were not sure how a garage door service would fit under their existing residential service offerings.

Unfortunately, what was presented was not what was delivered. The staff of Welborn did not share Milestone's morals or values. They didn't believe in Faith, Family, and Excellence. It was Milestone's largest acquisition to date, but it came with a lot of internal problems. Through intensive restructuring, Gus and Mark worked out the kinks and kept the Welborn name. It was now time to find someone to run that service line.

They asked Mike, a hardworking guy they knew from church, to come in. They asked him to see what they had done with the garage door service line. He was very interested in its potential. Gus and Mark hired Mike to take over Welborn and lead their team. It took some work to get things synced up, but to this day, every Welborn team member attends Milestone meetings. Two companies, two different names, one unified mission. Welborn now brings in over $13 million annually. This profitable acquisition happened simply because Gus and Mark were willing to give the original owner a little bit of their time.

Sometimes, meaningful relationships form just by taking a chance, like how Steve came to work at Milestone. Steve, a retired Marine, worked hard his whole life. He was meritoriously promoted to every rank attained and selected as one of only twenty Marines from a squadron of three hundred to participate in Desert Storm operations. Steve put himself through college, supported his family, and eventually secured a job as vice president of acquisitions at Dean Foods, a national food and beverage company. It was the corporate dream after a long climb to the top. Steve worked at Dean Foods for over twelve years.

As the story goes, Steve's wife Tammy and Gus's wife Amanda knew each other before Steve and Gus met. The men both lived in Heath, Texas, in Rockwall County and would bump into each other at neighborhood gatherings. Over several social gatherings, Gus and Steve got to know each other.

"It sounds like you're in a great spot, Steve," Gus said at a neighbor's barbecue in the spring of 2014.

"Yeah, it is all right. Does well with the family," Steve replied.

"You wouldn't want to come work with Milestone, would you?" Gus said, half joking.

He expected Steve to laugh and decline but was met by contemplative silence.

"If you're serious, I wouldn't mind talking about the opportunity," Steve replied.

"Oh, I am serious," Gus said quickly.

Little did Gus know that Steve was struggling with corporate burnout. His work environment, though lucrative, was unhealthy mentally, emotionally, and, above all, spiritually. Perhaps the same driving force that inspired Mark to ask Gus to work for him was working that evening in Heath. Steve met with Gus and Mark a few days later and agreed to take on the role of Milestone's chief financial officer.

Steve bleeds red and yellow. If you ask him, he will tell you without hesitation that this is the best job he has ever had. Steve finally feels a sense of purpose in his work beyond earning a paycheck. He enjoys his coworkers and the culture Milestone has spent years building and improving. Steve is an essential part of leadership development among the team and partner in affiliate businesses.

The most important asset in business is relationships. You can spend all of your money and time building the brand, improving productivity, and innovating processes, but success is strengthened in the network you create. Gus and Mark have spent their lives cultivating meaningful relationships, and some of those relationships have shaped the very existence of Milestone. Like Steve, many team members feel empowered by Milestone's greater purpose: to be the most impactful company in the Dallas–Fort Worth area.

United States veteran Steve Schultz, alongside other veteran brothers on the Milestone team

Milestone "Dunking Dads" at a community basketball event

Steve Boyle
Eric Martinez Rasheal Winters
Tim Cardoso Greg Wong Joe Blassingame Brien
Toombs Keith Abraham Michael Maxam Jordan Faith
Aaron Behunin Todd Dukes David Lozano Trey Cole Kambria
Robison Stephen Woods Jonathon Hallford Noe Cabrera Samantha
Bowden Sylvester Merkley Nikko Garcia Corey Walker Derek Bryant Tyler
Spears Bradley Christensen Yannete Duran Laura Robbins Kirstyn Blackwood
Nick Schilperoort Erik Puga Brandon Lemmon Joshua Segura Kirstie Kinsey Ja-
cob Steward Robert Webster Benjamin Baldwin Bobby Stiefer III Bradley Simpson
Nathan Gurera Haley Barrow Draven   Worden Gojko Ljumovic Daniel
Rojas Marcos Caldera Jr. Derrick   Robbins Joe Rhead Martin
Montelongo Alejundra Plancarte   Robert Hall Mario Silva Aaron
Wheeler James Holiday Tyler   Blann Christopher Storie Robert
Ricks David Steinc Danielle Smith   James Hacker Donald Spur-
lock Cameron Simmons Andres   Gonzales Jose A Padilla Austin
James Devin Ballard Kayla Far-   rias Christopher Bedford Jacob
Sessions John Zepeda Cameron   Ellis Ryan Fritz Sergio Salinas
Hunter Smith Jason Michaels Selena   Castillo Jonathan Velez Jose Silva
Mike Simon Ruben Anguiano Amber Peak Carlos Guzman Kimberly Graves
Kayce Douthit Grayson Lewis Chad Rodriguez Billy Wiginton Raul Ramirez
Daniel McCowen Omar Ramirez Andres Padilla Devin Morrow Jackie Wat-
kins Joe Sorrells Francisco Ramirez Anthony Esparza Alex Gonzalez
Daniel Gomez-Ramirez Corey Cantrell Alejandro Berber Jeff
Means Collin Gresso David Saunders Justin Braughler
Hayden Arnold Tyler Blume Nich-
olas Burris Allie Coppedge Hunter
Morgan Michael Barber Timothy
Lewis David Acebedo Andee Olivares
Wesley Zapata Nick Sessums Jacques
Franklin Robert Renfro Randy Car-
penter Adrian Salinas Dalton Stewart
Alyssa Fore John Capps Jesse Marti-
nez Jesse Morgan Jourdan Patterson

MAKE A PROFIT TO EXIST, DON'T EXIST TO PROFIT

**Give, and it will be given to you.
A good measure, pressed down, shaken
together and running over, will be poured
into your lap. For with the measure you
use, it will be measured to you.**

—Luke 6:38 NIV

No matter how successful a person becomes in business or in life, it is important to look for opportunities to better yourself and your organization. Never be "done." The work never ends. But remember, success doesn't depend on others having less. Maintain a giver's mentality, and doors to new opportunities will continue to open.

In 2014, Eric sent Gus and Mark an email about a program his mother's company had established for its employees. Each team member gave a small monthly or weekly amount of money to a general fund, and that fund was used to help team members and people in the community.

Gus and Mark talked it over and got inspired. They weren't sure what the response would be like if they rolled out something similar at Milestone. It was worth a try. With Eric's help, Gus and Mark presented the initiative to the Milestone family. Just about everyone jumped onboard and gave at least five dollars a week. The fund was named Milestone Cares.

Milestone Cares supports both team members in need and issues in the community. On one occasion, a technician's father passed away and he needed help with travel expenses. Milestone Cares helped that team member get to his family for the funeral. A Milestone team member lost her house when a tornado ravaged the area in 2016. Milestone Cares stepped in and filled the gap financially for her so she could rebuild her life. To this day, 90 percent of team members actively contribute on a weekly basis.

Always striving for impact, the Milestone team has found some incredible ways to make a difference in the community. In late 2016, Gus and Mark invited Ryan Leak, author of *Chasing Failure*, to present at a ten a.m. leadership meeting. Ryan talked about setting a goal so big that if you missed it, you'd still go further than you ever could. This goal had to have stipulations and deadlines to keep the goal chasers honest and motivated. It had to be measurable. As Ryan spoke, his words sent shockwaves throughout the room. The Milestone team would have a huge goal, but the catalyst for this idea happened a week prior.

It was September 2016 and Gus was flying home. A man sat next to him on the plane. As they took off, something shiny caught Gus's eye. The man was wearing a bracelet. Gus had seen this type of bracelet before. It was a piece of memorabilia honoring a fallen soldier. Gus, being Gus, decided to ask his seatmate about the bracelet and ultimately the passenger's military service.

Gus happened to be flying next to Major Dan Rooney, CEO and founder of Folds of Honor, an organization that provides educational scholarships to spouses and children of America's fallen and disabled service members. Gus was inspired by Major Rooney's story and wanted to give back to his organization. The seed was planted. One week later, after Ryan's talk, Gus approached Travis from marketing with a big idea.

"Travis, I want to raise a million dollars for Folds of Honor. Let's do it," Gus said.

"Oh, that is a big initiative," Travis said. "I'll get the team together."

Some of the Stand to Honor team that helped raise $1 million for children of fallen soldiers

Travis and the marketing team brainstormed the best way to raise the huge financial goal.

"How many car washes do you think that is?" Travis asked the group with a grin. They laughed.

It took months, but finally the team had a big idea. Milestone would host an event called Stand to Honor. Individuals would stand on thirteen wooden boxes twenty-four hours a day, seven days a week until they raised $1 million. Each box would have a plaque that read "Their selflessness, patriotism, and love for country will always be remembered." A set of soldier's boot prints would be pressed on the top of the box. Volunteers would literally be standing in the footsteps of fallen soldiers. The proceeds would go to Folds of Honor.

Travis and the marketing team deployed every tool they could think of. They reached out to SGI, other companies across the area, and every local media outlet. The team spent eight months preparing for the event, which would take place in May 2017 at Victory Plaza, downtown Dallas.

On the morning of May 6, Milestone team members donned blue t-shirts with a red "Stand to Honor" emblazoned on the front of them. Fox News came out to cover the kickoff, and the team raised $175,000 within the first day. Excited by the momentum, Gus, Mark, Travis, and everyone involved thought they'd hit $1 million within seventy-two hours.

Local celebrities came out and stood on the boxes. Awareness quickly grew. A family drove six hours from Joplin, Missouri, to participate. Local and national news outlets covered the team's efforts, and the project went viral. But it took a little more than seventy-two hours.

By day four, they had raised $450,000. Apparently, when doing a fundraiser of this magnitude, it is beneficial to raise about 60 percent of the funds before the main event. Unfortunately, Milestone raised zero dollars prior to the event. Lesson learned. The team had only envisioned a three-day event, but the turnout remained strong. Families who lost loved ones came to stand for hours at a time. Active duty military personnel came to stand in honor of fallen friends. Morning, noon, and night, rain or shine, people were standing. Truthfully, Travis never counted on other people outside of the Milestone family to participate. It was unforgettable to see people from all over the area spend time with the team.

Stand to Honor continued through Mother's Day weekend. Gus and Mark offered to take a break so their wives could enjoy a nice Mother's Day brunch, but the women refused—Amanda and Sabrina insisted on standing. They knew mothers of fallen soldiers would be standing that day. They were joined by a bunch of mothers from Milestone. Amanda stood for nearly twenty-four hours. It was a Mother's Day she will never forget.

Milestone technicians came to stand on the boxes. The accounting department took shifts. Just about every pair of feet employed by Milestone spent time on the Stand to Honor boxes. By day seven, they raised $600,000. Momentum started to slow down, news teams left to cover other stories, but the team kept standing.

It got to the point where Gus considered writing a check for the difference to end the initiative. He wanted everyone to celebrate their success and return to their families. Instead of flowing in, donations slowed to a trickle.

The goal seemed further away than ever.

"Let's pray about it," Travis said, and they did. The team decided to stand for a few more days. They weren't ready to give up.

A day later, Baltimore Orioles first baseman Chris Davis sent in a $50,000 donation. The team started freaking out. It was the break they needed when they were so close to giving up. This was the sign they needed to keep on standing. The news vans returned in droves. Meteorologist Pete Delkus and others began delivering weather reports at Victory Plaza, and anchors led live broadcasts with updates each morning and evening. Then another $50,000 donation came through.

Companies started offering to match any donation that came through within the next twelve hours. Donations poured in throughout the night. Then, finally, on the thirteenth day, Milestone hit the $1 million goal. They chased failure and found success.

Eric smiled as Travis, Gus, and Mark burst into applause. Cheers could be heard throughout the area as the crowd burst into a rendition of the national anthem. Each and every Milestone team member was in awe of their accomplishment. To think they almost quit halfway through only to see their "impossible" goal come to fruition. Thirteen days and nights were spent in the Dallas sun (and rain). Countless strangers became friends as they stood on top of the boxes, sharing stories of the motivation behind their journey to the event. Veterans and service dogs dutifully honored fallen comrades. It was an unforgettable experience for every soul involved.

Stand to Honor served as inspiration for the Milestone team to create a new nonprofit organization called 19 Ministries. This nonprofit would allow the team to be more strategic with the money they give to charities, churches, and communities. The goal was to "laser beam" financial and volunteer resources into a single community to make a lasting impact over time instead of sprinkling resources across communities. Rowlett, Texas, a local neighborhood with a large school-age population, was chosen first.

19 Ministries was founded in spring 2018 with the vision to impact cities in the Dallas–Fort Worth area. The board is made up of pastors and businessmen who desire to see God's love impact cities. Milestone is a key partner, and Gus and Mark sit on the board. Milestone team members are active in the organization's community efforts.

All of this is a testimony to the faithfulness to God. It is paramount to have faith when you're struggling, but it is equally important to have faith when you're successful. Milestone is a conduit to impact. It doesn't exist to profit; it simply profits to exist and be a blessing to as many as possible. After all, Milestone has received many blessings along the way.

Supporting first responders who serve and protect our community

*Milestone team members volunteering time on the
weekend to work with Habitat for Humanity*

*Milestone gifted a Disney trip giveaway to a first-responder
family nominated by a friend or family!*

Dante Marsaw George Putnam Michael Walker Levi Taylor Matthew Milam Allan Shocknesse Britton Swanson Madison Severn JR McAuley Sydney Mouton Geoff Gage Jeff Crouse Brian Cline Antonio Canales Jay Conley Emma Thieman Matt Jacob Dylan Tigert Russell Patterson Dakota Worley Savannah Moore Derek McClendon Charles Crapo Scott Menzies Jake Waide Adam Tims Dontay Worden Alister Smith Alexander Gonzales Marcus Lynch Toby Worley Travon Marsaw Ralph Garrett Riley Cole Bethany Weisser Jenna Drane Jasmine McGuire Ty Crook Riley Stratton Clark Stewart Harlan Haire Bewar Ali Alan Sykes Hanna Jones Bobby Wickersham Clint Codling Jose Maldonado Emilio Patella Chance Walter Joey Renfro Jay Henderson George Rasugu Hayley Copeland Mike Wheeler Jasper Pitrello Libby Reynolds Jose Posada Syres Whitfield

Aaron Cicero Ryan Oden Mitch Kilbride Timothy Haggerty Adam Hall Kasey Hungerford Dillon Collard Chris Thompson Destiny Torres Nathan Hager Courtney Pritchard Mike Castillo Mike Edwards Pablo Gaspar Kaitlyn Stinson Tadeo Gonzalez Jonathan Henshaw Jesse Fagan Kirk Rouse Travis Whitt Gilbert Mendez Travis Franklin Nicole Brown Jared Fitzgerald Jonathan Nobles Jose Mejia chez Alejandro Aguila tis Tyler Herriage Bryan Holly Mapel Karis Evick Renner Brandyn Brewer Roach Patrick McCauley Guerrero Mark Medeiros Thomas Edith Marti- Garza Caleb Hessert Warren Cassandra Mc- Brittani Gords Jake Silvio Israel Diaz Shawn Isbell Alexander Patrick Deren Sorrells Jeremiah Hollo- pinoza Kelsi Mata Keane Tomei Oscar Velasquez Patrick Mc- Craw Johnathan Perry Hunter Sullivan Chris Reyes Darrell Sanders Caylin Ketchum Hannah Morel Anna Hicks Angel Lindert Akuri Ndamukong Dylan Bray-Rosales Dale Ladd Alan Grussendorf Cristoval Ingram Ira Houston Randall Tadlock Scott Moore Johnny Rivera Baldemar Arreola Chris Gibson Justin Sadler Felipe Carbajal

Alex Arenas Nelson San- Steve Pound Steven Cur- Seckinger Bryan Serrano Steven Becker Reed Charlie De Santiago Tim Levi Coppedge Juan Zac Cranford Josalyn nez Obed Cisneros Jose Kaeci Story Breanna Cauley Brittany Palmer Dalton Chase Colt Cash Ronny Stidham Elisha Juanita Muniz Andrew way Colby Adams Julio Es-

BEING A GOOD STEWARD

In everything I did, I showed you that by this kind of hard work we must help the weak, remembering the words the LORD Jesus himself said: "It is more blessed to give than to receive."

—*Acts 20:35 NIV*

Two Thousand One Hundred Seventy Six

Gus and Mark believe God has given them the tools, resources, and people to create and run Milestone. They know they have been entrusted with a business that team members and customers depend on. To them, this means making decisions for the people rather than for themselves.

"People Serving People" slide displayed at every leadership meeting, reminding the team that serving our people and their families is top priority!

When making a small departmental decision or a large corporate-wide decision, the leaders at Milestone discuss the sixteen hundred. Every decision considered and change made directly impacts sixteen hundred people. This number represents the total number of Milestone team members and their family members. The marketing team developed a slide with photos of team members and families as a visual reminder for meetings. This sentiment trickles down to personal decisions as well. It challenges team members to ask themselves, "What kind of example am I setting for the people on my team?" This internal check-in fosters a sense of self-awareness that benefits everyone at Milestone.

Gus and Mark have built a faith-based culture that values team members' passion, talent, and, above all, time. From the company breakfasts to the ninety-day check-ins to every little personalized touchpoint in between, Milestone invests everything in its people. Gus and Mark have heard stories of team members who decided to get Milestone logo tattoos because they believe in their work and love what they do so much!

Mark C. (a.k.a. Milestone Mark) is such a famous presence in the community, he brings breakfast or lunch to area fire stations, police headquarters, nursing homes, and schools. He checks in to see what community needs they might have and reports back to Milestone so the team can determine ways they can help. It is one way Milestone can serve better.

The Milestone team embraces the visibility the company has in the immediate community. Customers have requested to borrow Milestone technician uniforms for children's Halloween costumes. They have mailed in photos of Milestone-themed birthday cakes. The team has even received disgruntled calls from parents because their children won't stop singing the Milestone commercial jingle. These small moments of recognition really speak to how impactful Milestone truly is.

Then there are the big moments of recognition.

"Mark, check this out," Gus said in the summer of 2010. "You aren't gonna believe this."

"What's up?"

"According to this letter, Milestone has been named as one of the fastest growing companies in the Dallas–Fort Worth area by Southern Methodist University (SMU). We're in the SMU Dallas 100!"

"Wow!" Mark said. "I can't believe it."

"The award ceremony is in November."

"Can we bring guests?"

"Looks like it."

"How about we invite Pastor Mike and his wife?" Mark suggested. "We owe a lot to them and the church for getting Milestone to where it is today."

"That is a great idea. Give them a call. Here is the information."

Gus and Mark have always given credit where credit is due, but that award gave Gus and Mark a real sense of accomplishment. The pair didn't have college degrees, and yet a prestigious university with one of the best business schools in the south recognized Milestone—one of the few companies on the list with primarily blue-collar workers—for its growth.

Mark and Gus received a beautiful glass award at the recognition dinner. As they returned to the table, Mike smiled.

"Congratulations, Gus and Mark," Mike said. "Next Sunday, I'd love for you two to come on stage and share your story with our parishioners. You can really speak to the goodness of God."

Neither Gus nor Mark relished public speaking, but they hesitantly agreed. A typical Sunday service at their church had nearly fifteen hundred parishioners.

As they wrote down talking points a few nights before the service, they happened upon a great idea. Gus and Mark would bring the glass award, tell the Milestone story, and then present the award to Mike and their church. They wanted to credit the foundation of faith their church gave them during the hardest times of growing the business.

Looking back at that momentous lunch at Joe Willy's, fifteen years before, when they weren't yet partners, Mark posed a question to Gus before they became partners.

"What are your goals in life?" Mark asked.

"I just want to do something meaningful," Gus replied.

"Well, what are your financial goals? What is the most amount of money you ever thought you could make in the future?"

"Man, if I could ever make like $80,000 a year, I think that would be incredible. But if it doesn't happen, I won't be devastated," Gus offered.

And it happened.

From: JONATHAN C PHILLIPS
Sent: Monday, February 17, 2020 1:20 PM
To: Constantine "Gus" Antos
Subject: Gratitude

Gus,

I wanted to take a second to say thank you for the impact you've had on my life.

I hadn't understood what dignity was when I sat down in that little office, just off Rowlett Road. I had no clue what I was getting myself into. All I knew is that I had $650 to my name, and I would do anything to keep my family together. We'd just moved from Ocean Springs, MS. I'd been a college pastor and worship leader in the wake of Hurricane Katrina, through the Housing Market Crash of 2008, and during the BP oil spill that devastated so many industries on the coast. I didn't have a job. My wife made $750 a month after taxes. We cashed our last check, hopped in the car, and drove the ten-hour drive from the Gulf Coast to Mesquite. The day I walked in for my interview at Milestone, I felt like I was walking into a Sunday church service. Everyone was incredibly nice. Maybe it was more like walking into the house of a family who had just adopted me.

Fast-forward to the day I decided that I wanted to buy a house. I remember walking into Missy's office and telling her that I wanted to take on-call [assignments] whenever I could. It was so amazing and encouraging, being part of a team that cheered me on and watched as I grinned like I never had before. And the day that I bought my house, I wanted to show it off to my Milestone family. And then you, Gus, you sent techs to my house to make sure it felt like home. Well, to this day, it is still home.

I now travel and do customer service training in the home services industry for a living. Every time I get out of an Uber after a long trip home, I always pause, look at my home, and thank God. I thank God that my home is safe. I think Him that my home is always comfortable. I thank Him that it's secure so that I have peace of mind that my two little girls will be okay. I thank my God for you, Gus. You may never truly know the impact you had on my family, my self-esteem, and my destiny. I live a great life. I aspire to be great. I have decided to win. That's thanks to the messenger that my God sent me, you. God bless you.

An email that says it all

Gus and Mark never set out to build a $100 million company together, but they both enjoyed serving people, be they customers, the team, or the community. They believed in the same values, worked hard, and did an incredible job. Gus and Mark could easily sell Milestone and ride off into the sunset to do something more fun than work on people's ceiling fans and AC units. However, Gus will be the first to tell you he loves the business and enjoys getting up and coming into work every day. Gus and Mark believe in building and continuing Milestone so the kids of the current team members can one day look at the company and want to be a part of it.

Gus and Mark wanted a company that would make a difference. They want team members to be the best they can be and customers to have the best experience possible. They want Milestone to be an agent of change. Some people say a business's entire goal is to build it up so you can sell it, make a bunch of money, and never work again. If Gus and Mark did sell, they wouldn't cease working. They would take that money and do the exact same thing somewhere else because they feel that's their responsibility. The Bible doesn't say, "Be fruitful, multiply, and relax for the rest of your life."

Being good stewards isn't just about being trusted with what you have; it's also about developing resources for the next generation. Be a good steward of your time and your gifts. Remember, givers gain. Business isn't about making enough money to do nothing. It is about making enough money to do *something*.

The Milestone story is simply about the way Milestone's team members live, work, and serve. Every single person who dons a Milestone uniform, answers a Milestone customer call, wears a Milestone nametag, drives a Milestone truck, or distributes a Milestone business card has the incredible opportunity to come in contact with tens of thousands of people every year. Milestone's legacy tells a story about enriching the lives of everyone team members encounter. That legacy is built upon the motivation to leave every customer feeling confident, encouraged, and satisfied. As Milestone continues to grow, the team continues to broaden its reach and deepen Milestone's impact on the community.

"His master replied, 'Well done, good and faithful servant! You have been faithful with a few things; I will put you in charge of many things. Come and share your master's happiness!'" (Matthew 25:23 NIV).

THE END

ABOUT THE AUTHORS

In 2004 Mark Robison and Gus Antos cofounded Milestone Electric, a home service company that has since grown to over five hundred team members. Milestone has been awarded countless honors, including SMU Business School of Cox "Top 100" and Dallas Morning News Best Places to Work, but the organization is most distinguished for the six hundred thousand (and growing) customers served across the Dallas–Fort Worth metroplex.

Mark lives in Rockwall, Texas, with his wife Sabrina. They are proud parents to three children, Justin, Danielle, and Amanda, whose wonderful spouses are Kambria, Austin, and Gus!

Yes, Gus married Mark's oldest daughter, Amanda, in 2007. Gus and Amanda live in Heath, Texas, and are proud parents to sons Dean and Alexander.

Mark and Gus continue to develop the expansive vision for the Milestone enterprise, all in an effort to serve and influence the greater Dallas–Fort Worth community in the name of Jesus Christ.

THE CHARGE

We hope you enjoyed hearing about our short journey. Our desire is that these stories will inspire you in your own adventure. First, we hope that, after reading this book, anyone considering joining the Milestone team will gain a better understanding of who we are and what we value. Second, we hope you are able to learn a few things you can implement in your personal journey. Finally, we hope this book will encourage others trying to live a life of purpose, passion, servanthood, and faith. Just knowing there are others out there fighting the same fight has always been an encouragement to us. Whether you are just getting on the path or you are a little further down the road, we are all on the journey together, pushing and pulling each other along.

We challenge you to join us in doing your best to live with passion, listen to your childlike faith, be relentless, embrace your uniqueness, and view every part of your life—including your profession—as an opportunity to enrich others.

We all live two lives. The second one starts when we realize
we only have one. —Tom Hiddleston

All comments and questions are welcome.
gus@callmilestone.com
mark@callmilestone.com